FOR ORGANS, PIANOS & ELECTRONIC KEYBOARDS

E-Z PLAY® TODAY

402

the **20th Century** Broadway

D1144159

ISBN 0-634-02201-6

HAL•LEONARD®
CORPORATION

7777 W. BLUEMOUND RD. P.O. BOX 13819 MILWAUKEE, WI 53213

Visit Hal Leonard Online at
www.halleonard.com

CONTENTS

As If We Never Said Goodbye

from SUNSET BOULEVARD

Registration 2
Rhythm: Ballad or 8-Beat

Music by Andrew Lloyd Webber
Lyrics by Don Black and Christopher Hampton,
with contributions by Amy Powers

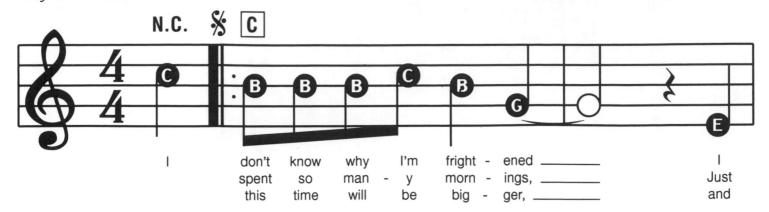

I
don't know why I'm fright - ened _____ I
spent so man - y morn - ings, _____ Just
this time will be big - ger, _____ and

know my way a - round here. _____ The card - board trees, the
try - ing to re - sist you. _____ I'm trem - bling now, you
bright - er than we knew it. _____ So watch me fly, we

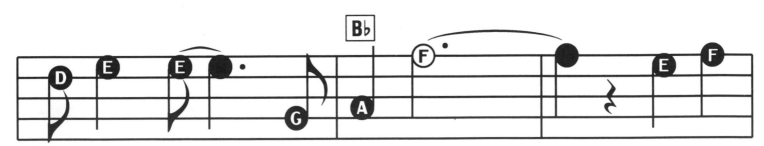

paint - ed seas, ___ the sound here. _____ Yes, a
can't know how ___ I've missed you, _____ missed the
all know I ___ can do it. _____ Could I

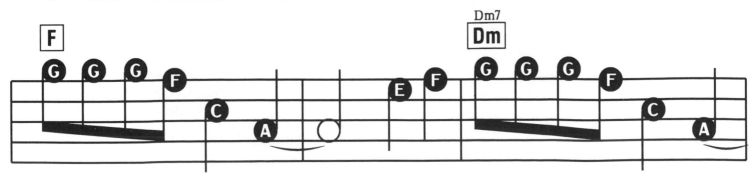

world to re - dis - cov - er, _____ but I'm not in an - y hur - ry, _____
fair - y tale ad - ven - tures _____ in this ev - er - spin - ning play - ground. _____
stop my hand from shak - ing? _____ Has there ev - er been a mo - ment

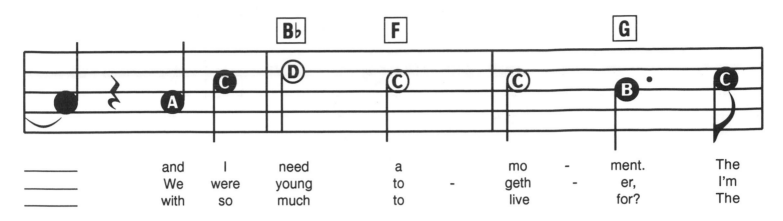

and I need a mo - ment. The
We were young to - geth - er, I'm
with so much to live for? The

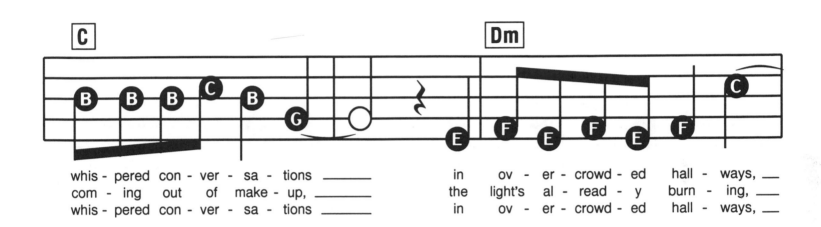

whis - pered con - ver - sa - tions _____ in ov - er - crowd - ed hall - ways, __
com - ing out of make - up, _____ the light's al - read - y burn - ing, __
whis - pered con - ver - sa - tions _____ in ov - er - crowd - ed hall - ways, __

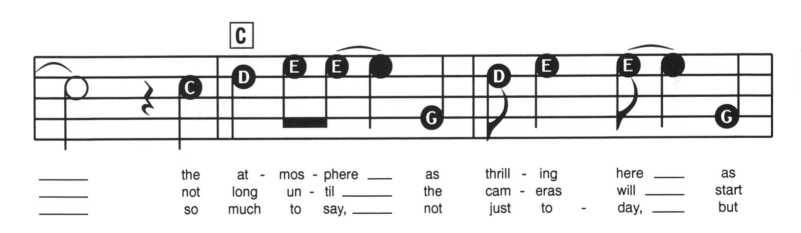

the at - mos - phere ___ as thrill - ing here ___ as
not long un - til _____ the cam - eras will _____ start
so much to say, _____ not just to - day, _____ but

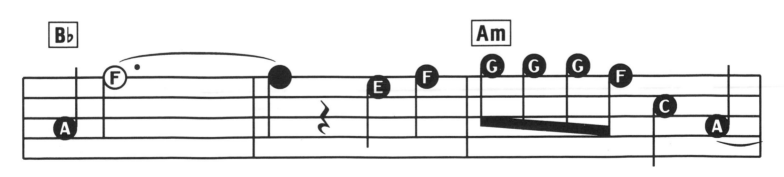

al - ways. _____ Feel the ear - ly morn - ing mad - ness, __
turn - ing, _____ and the ear - ly morn - ing mad - ness __
al - ways. _____ We'll have ear - ly morn - ing mad - ness, __

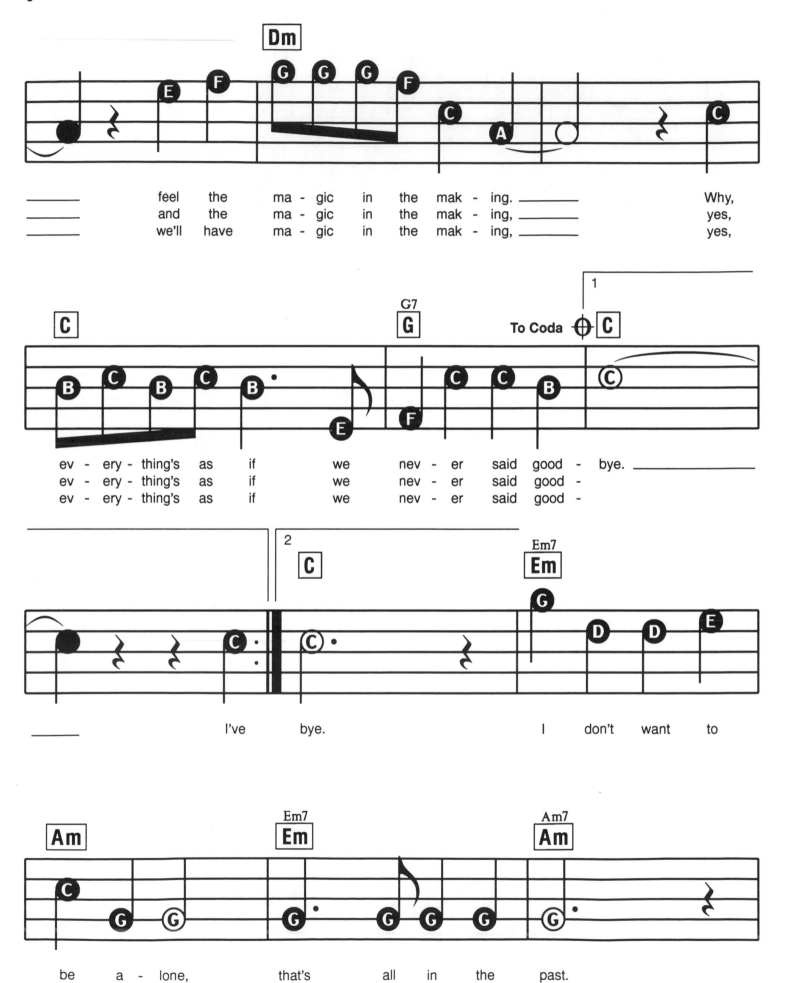

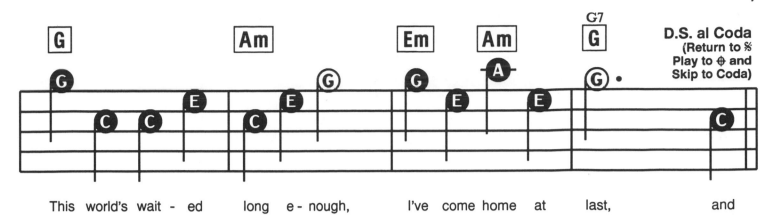

D.S. al Coda
(Return to %
Play to ⊕ and
Skip to Coda)

This world's wait - ed long e - nough, I've come home at last, and

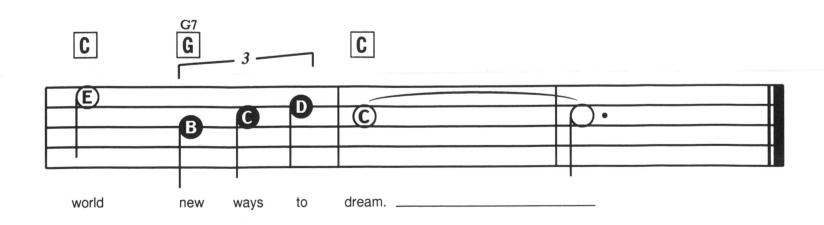

CODA

bye, _____ yes, ev - ery - thing's as if we

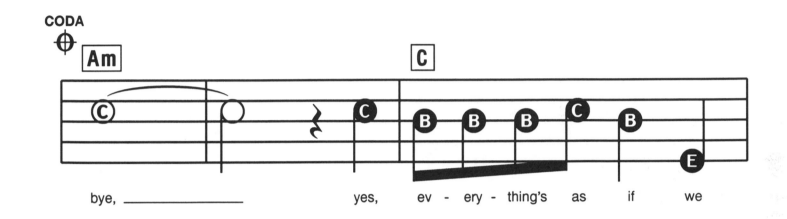

nev - er said good - bye. _____ We taught the

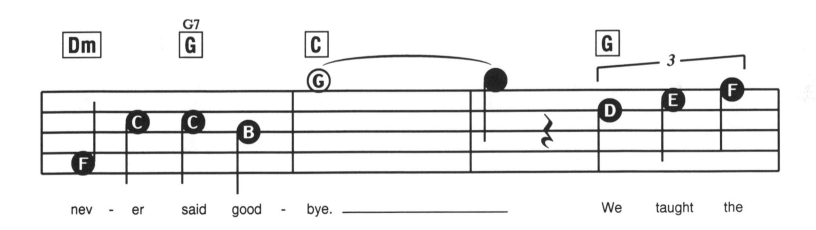

world new ways to dream. _____

Beauty and the Beast

from Walt Disney's BEAUTY AND THE BEAST: THE BROADWAY MUSICAL

Registration 1
Rhythm: Pops or 8 Beat

Lyrics by Howard Ashman
Music by Alan Menken

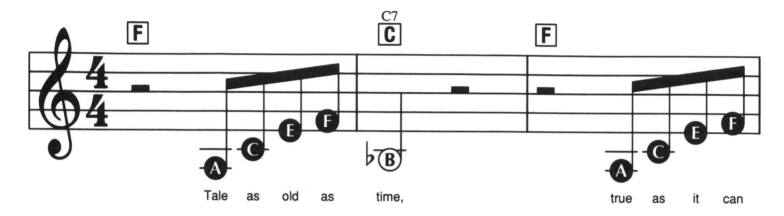

Tale as old as time, true as it can

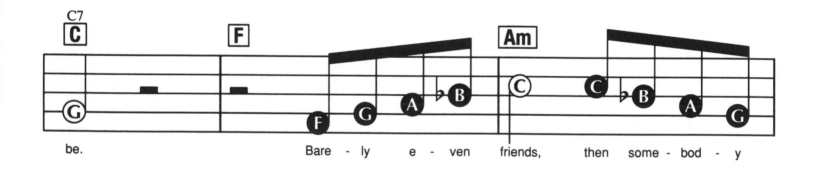

be. Bare - ly e - ven friends, then some - bod - y

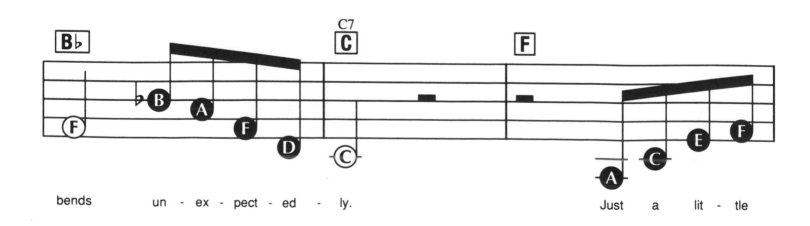

bends un - ex - pect - ed - ly. Just a lit - tle

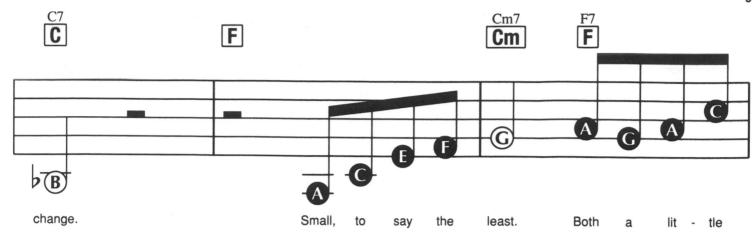

change. Small, to say the least. Both a lit - tle

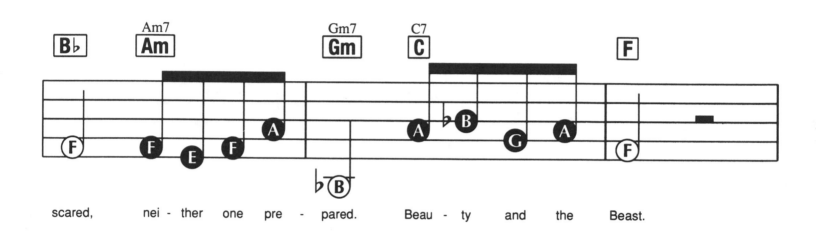

scared, nei - ther one pre - pared. Beau - ty and the Beast.

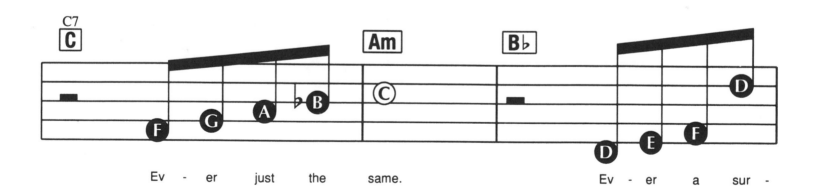

Ev - er just the same. Ev - er a sur -

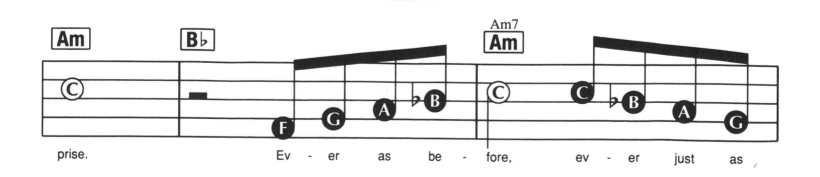

prise. Ev - er as be - fore, ev - er just as

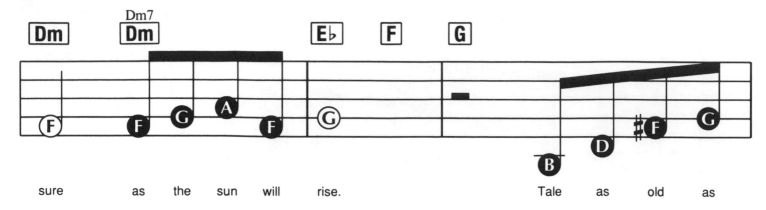

sure   as   the   sun   will   rise.   Tale   as   old   as

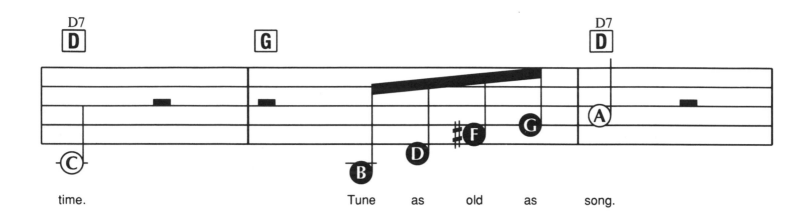

time.   Tune   as   old   as   song.

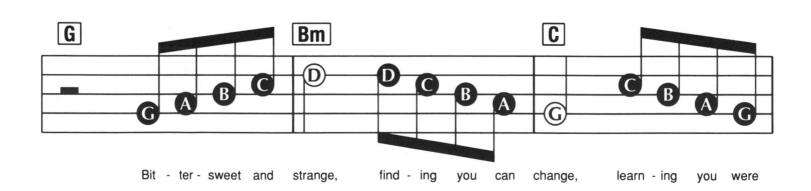

Bit - ter - sweet   and   strange,   find - ing   you   can   change,   learn - ing   you   were

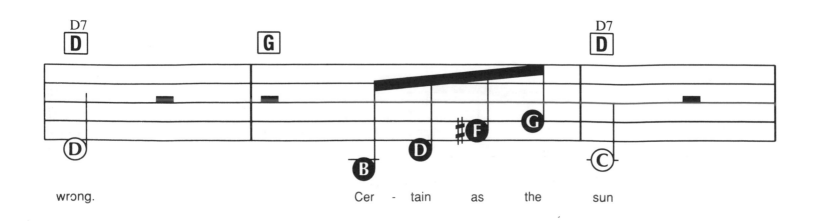

wrong.   Cer - tain   as   the   sun

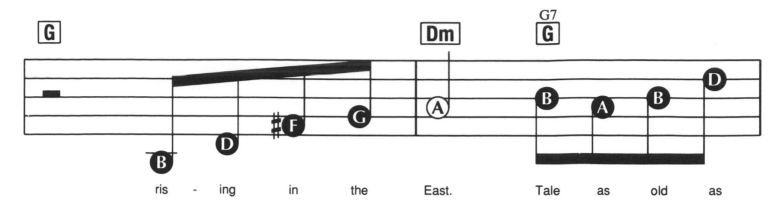

ris - ing in the East. Tale as old as

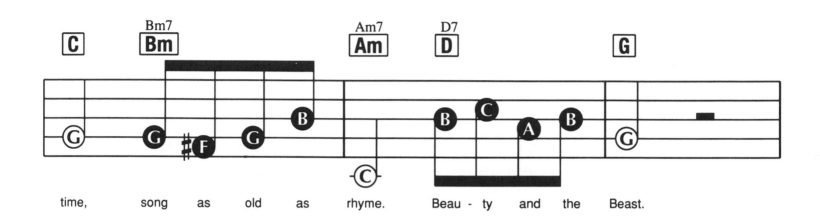

time, song as old as rhyme. Beau - ty and the Beast.

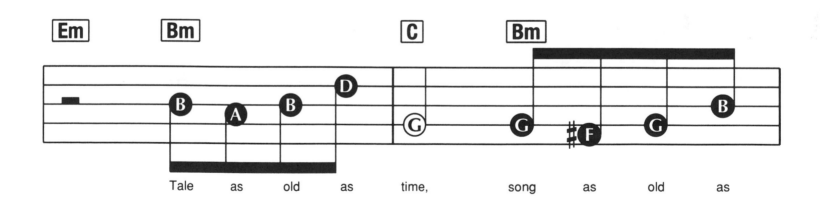

Tale as old as time, song as old as

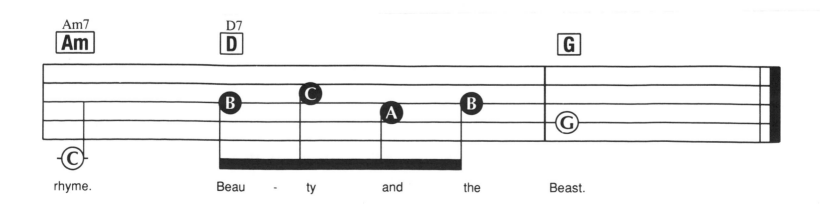

rhyme. Beau - ty and the Beast.

Bring Him Home
from LES MISÉRABLES

Registration 1
Rhythm: Ballad

Music by Claude-Michel Schönberg
Lyrics by Herbert Kretzmer and Alain Boublil

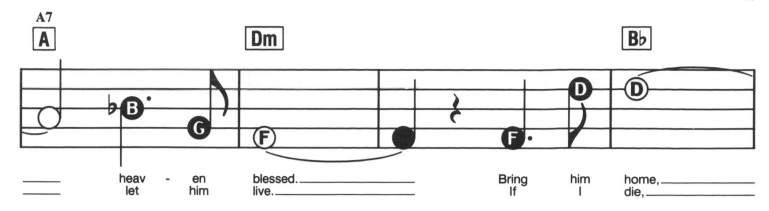

heav - en blessed. _____ Bring him home, _____
let him live. _____ If I die,

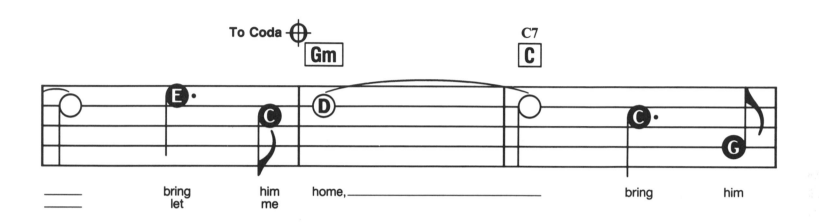

bring him home, _____ bring him
let me

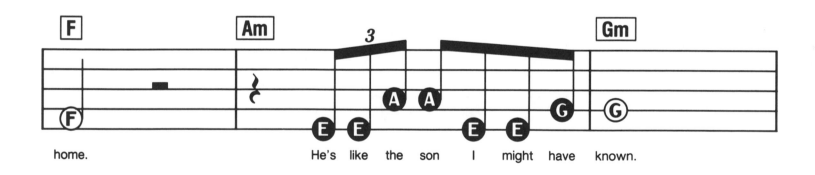

home. He's like the son I might have known.

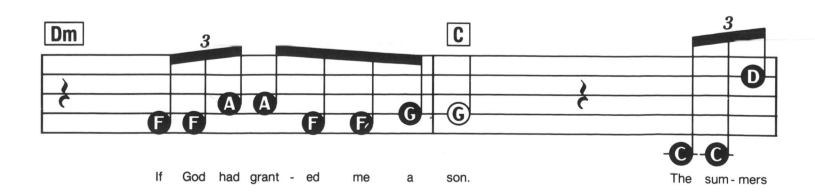

If God had grant - ed me a son. The sum - mers

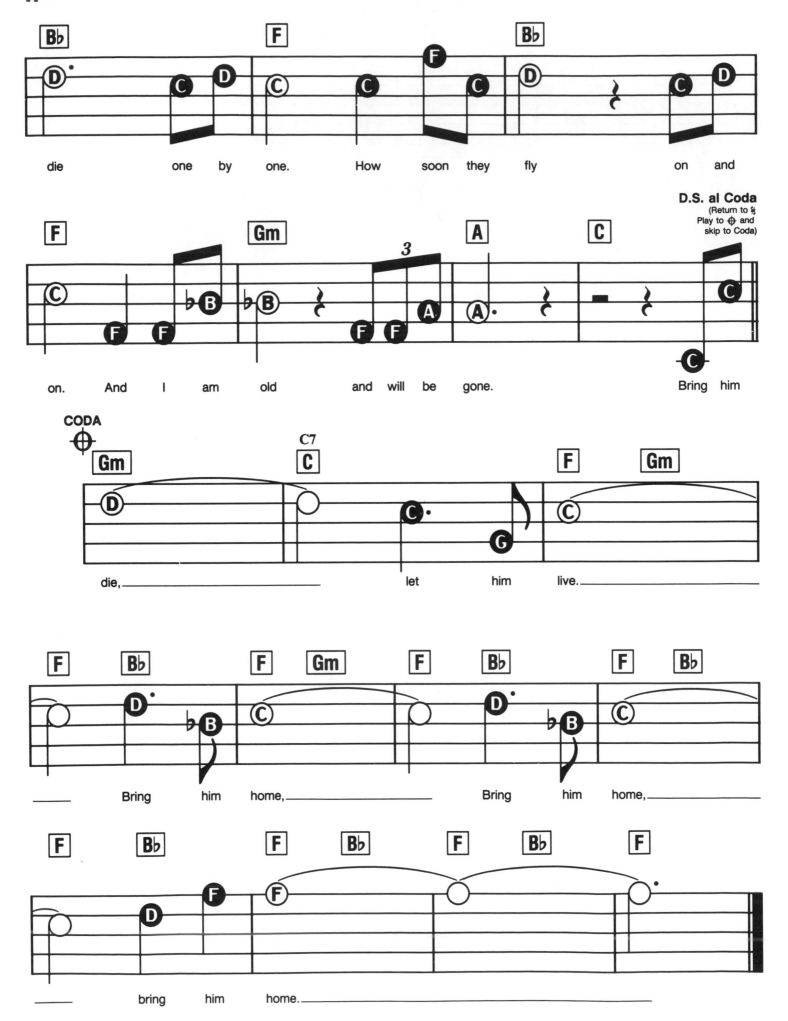

Cabaret
from the Musical CABARET

Registration 4
Rhythm: Fox Trot or Swing

Words by Fred Ebb
Music by John Kander

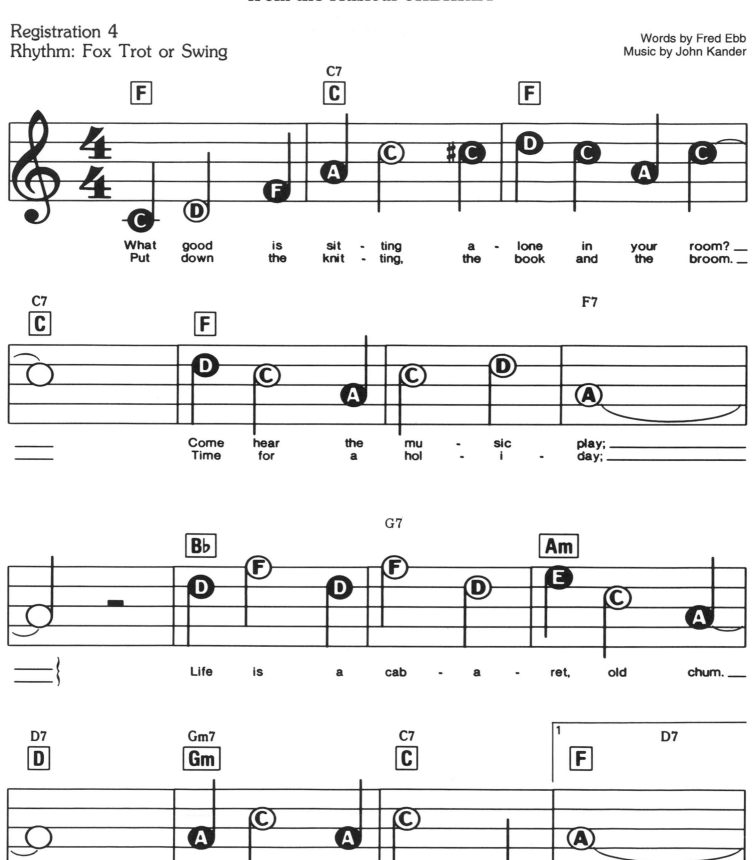

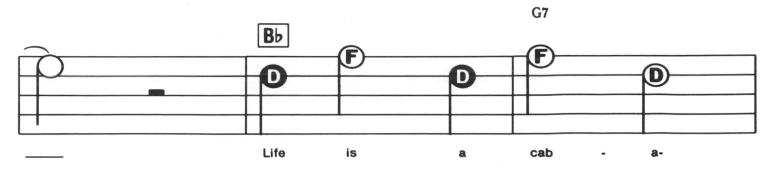

Life is a cab-a-

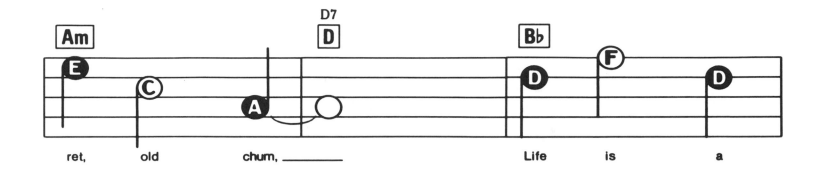

ret, old chum, _____ Life is a

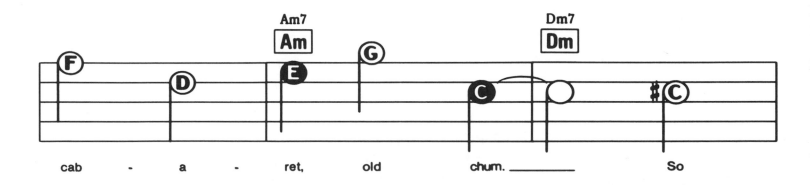

cab - a - ret, old chum. _____ So

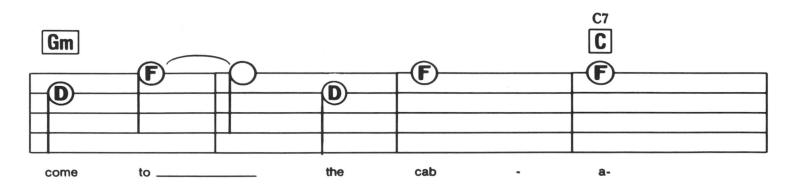

come to _____ the cab - a-

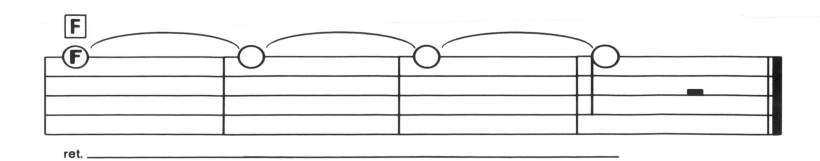

ret. _____

Brotherhood of Man
from HOW TO SUCCEED IN BUSINESS WITHOUT REALLY TRYING

Registration 5
Rhythm: Fox Trot or Polka

By Frank Loesser

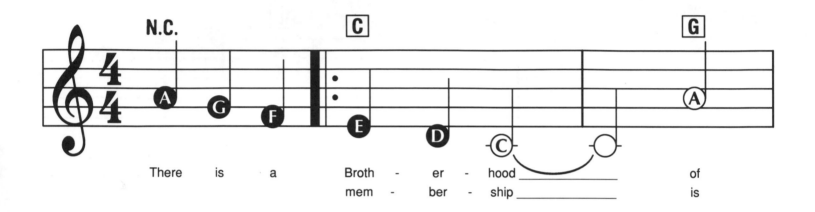

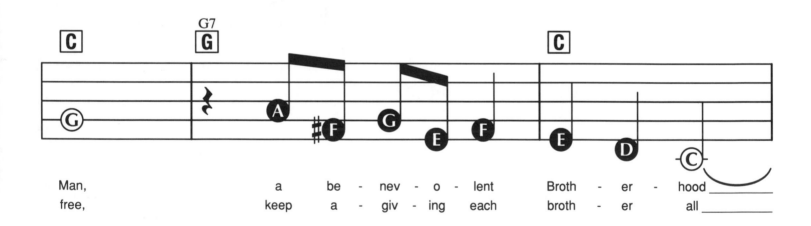

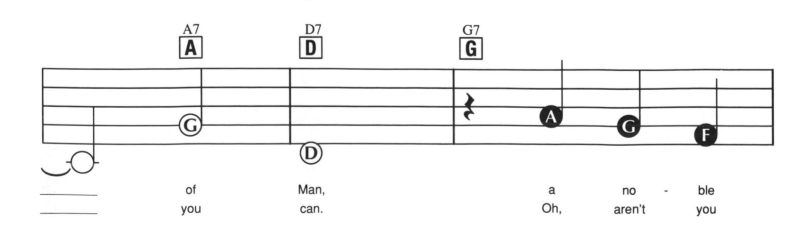

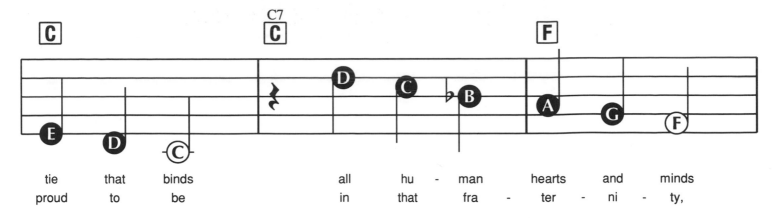

tie that binds all hu - man hearts and minds
proud to be in that fra - ter - ni - ty,

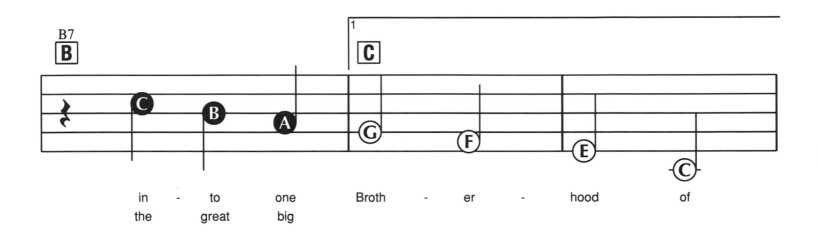

in - to one Broth - er - hood of
the great big

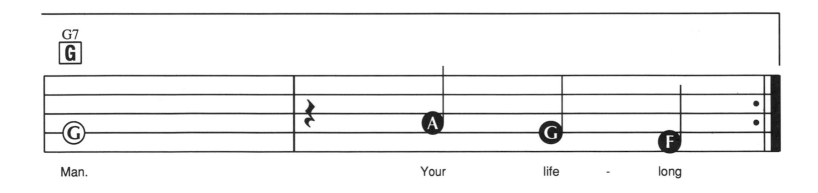

Man. Your life - long

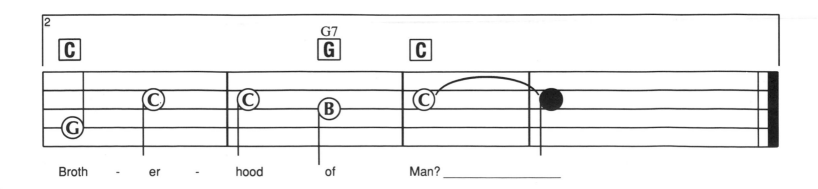

Broth - er - hood of Man? _____

Close Every Door
from JOSEPH AND THE AMAZING TECHNICOLOR® DREAMCOAT

Registration 2
Rhythm: Waltz

Music by Andrew Lloyd Webber
Lyrics by Tim Rice

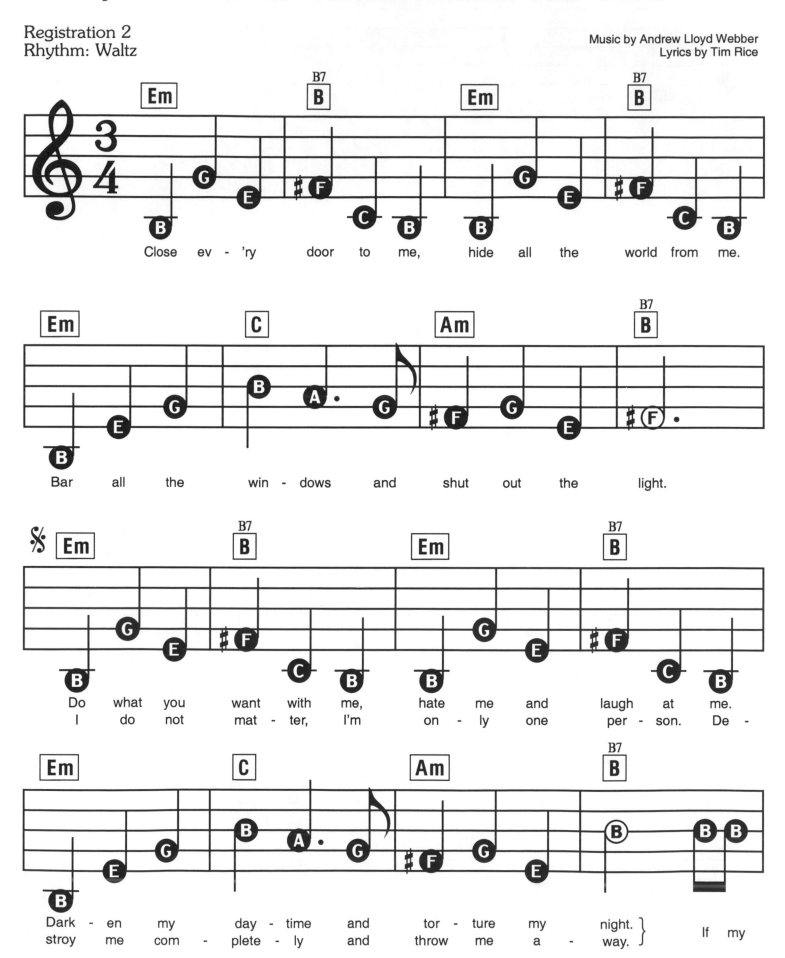

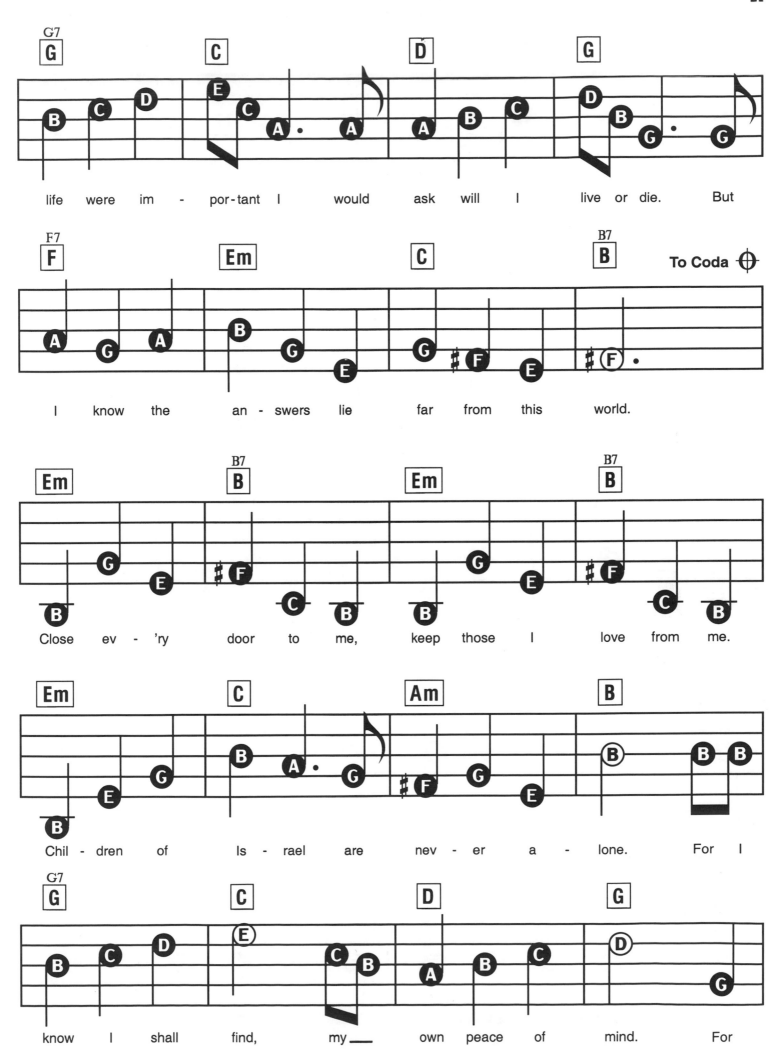

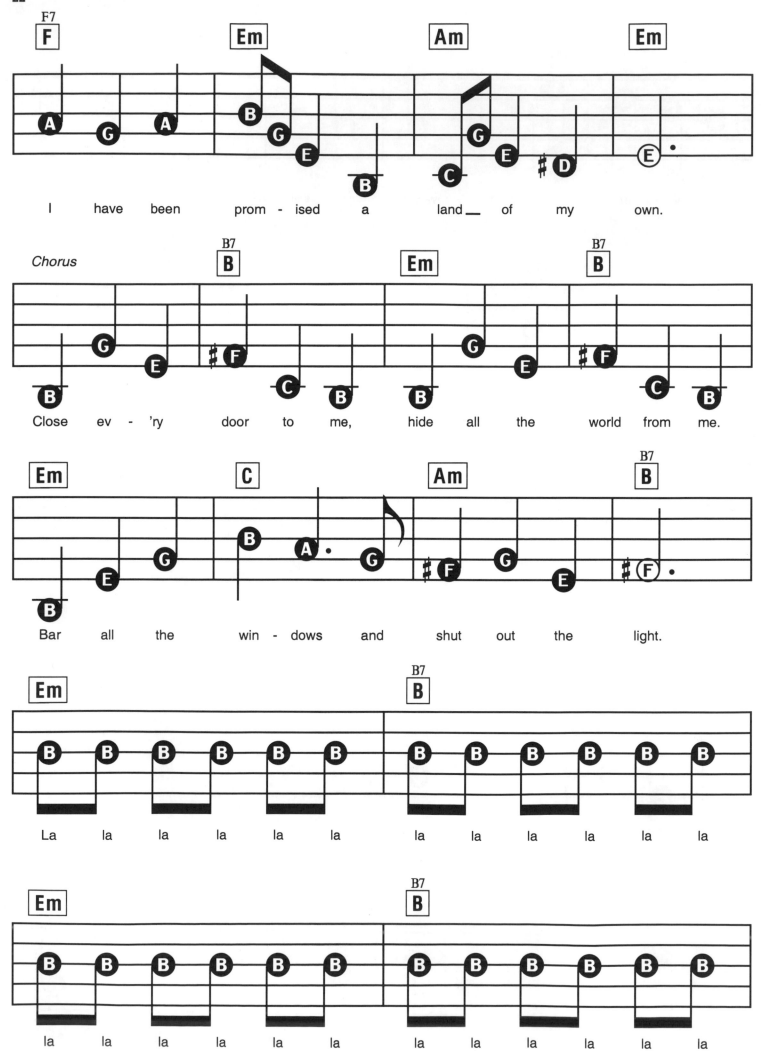

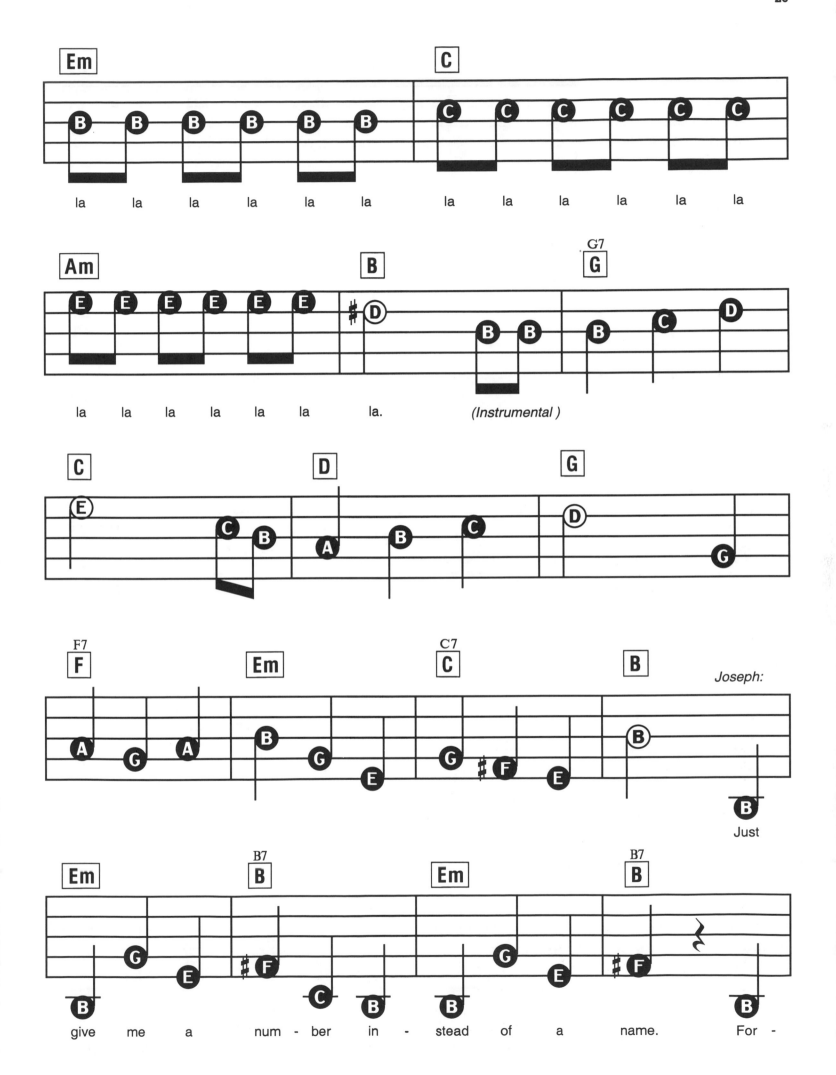

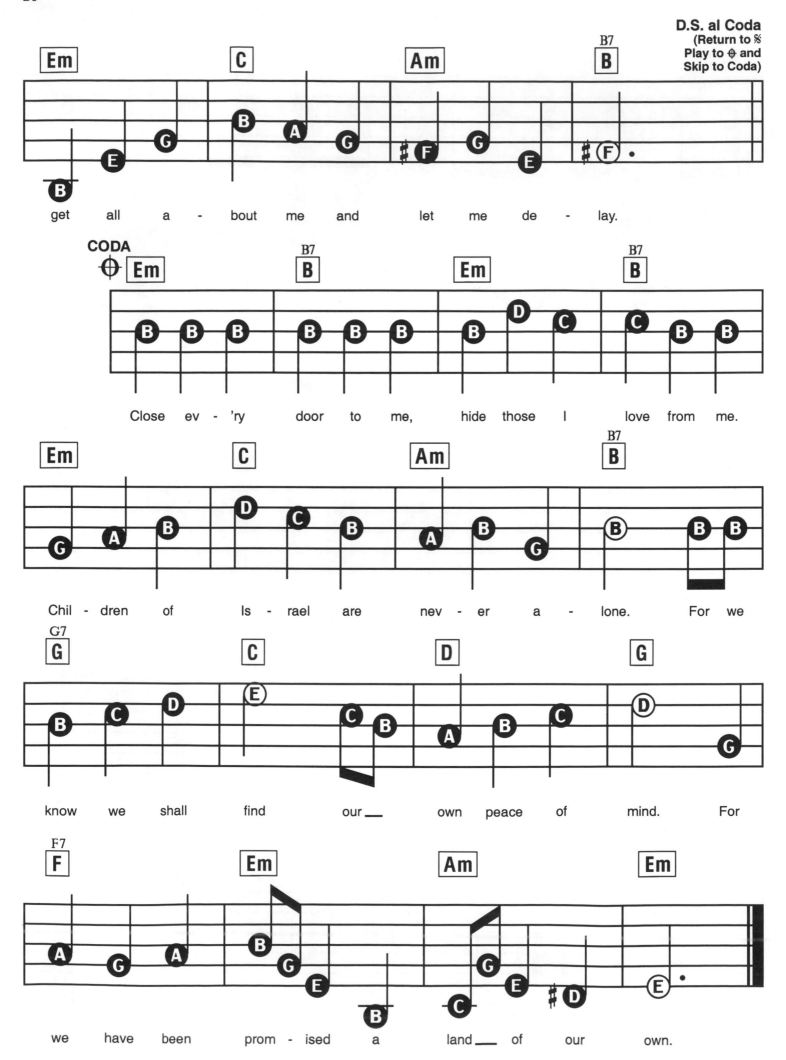

D.S. al Coda
(Return to %
Play to ⊕ and
Skip to Coda)

Comedy Tonight
from A FUNNY THING HAPPENED ON THE WAY TO THE FORUM

Registration 2
Rhythm: March or Polka

Words and Music by
Stephen Sondheim

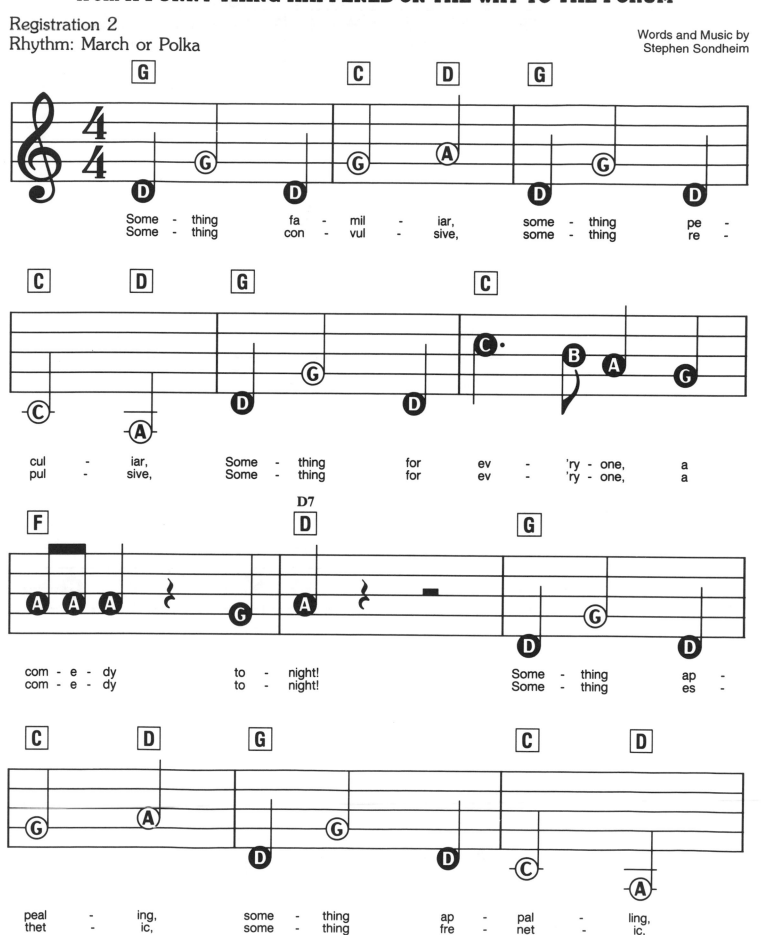

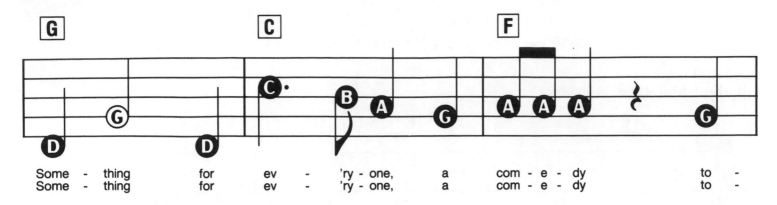

Some - thing for ev - 'ry - one, a com - e - dy to -
Some - thing for ev - 'ry - one, a com - e - dy to -

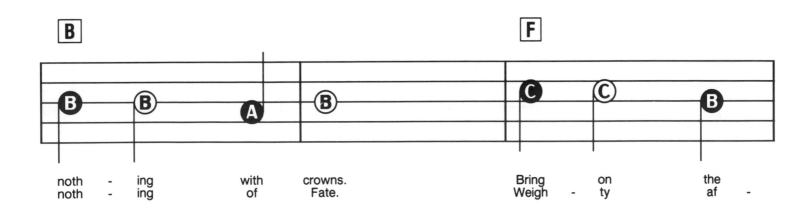

night! Noth - ing with kings,
night! Noth - ing of Gods,

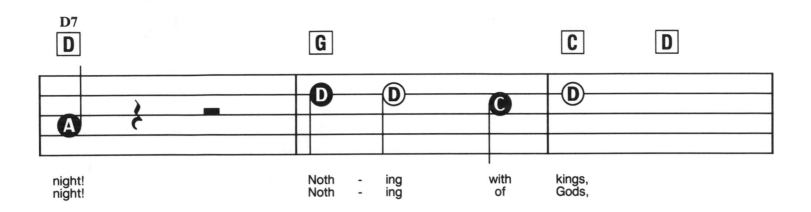

noth - ing with crowns. Bring on the
noth - ing of Fate. Weigh - ty af -

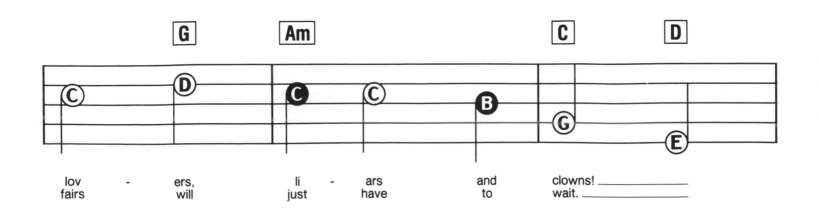

lov - ers, li - ars and clowns! _____
fairs will just have to wait. _____

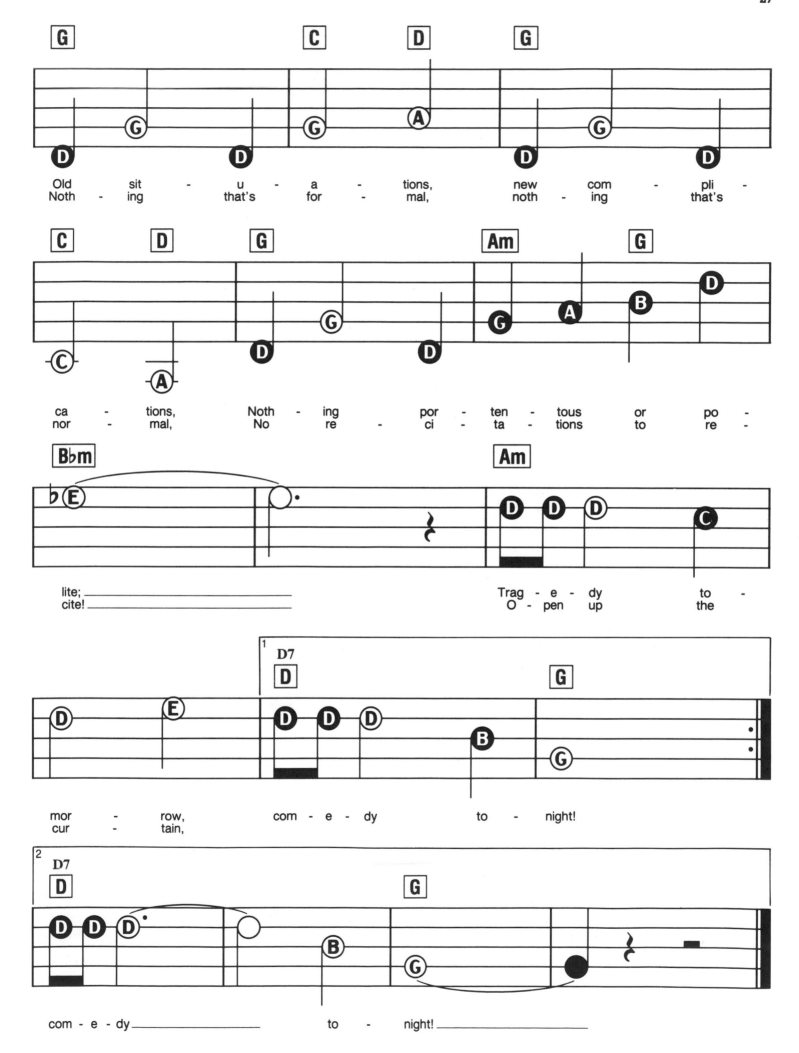

Do-Re-Mi
from THE SOUND OF MUSIC

Registration 4
Rhythm: Fox Trot or March

Lyrics by Oscar Hammerstein II
Music by Richard Rodgers

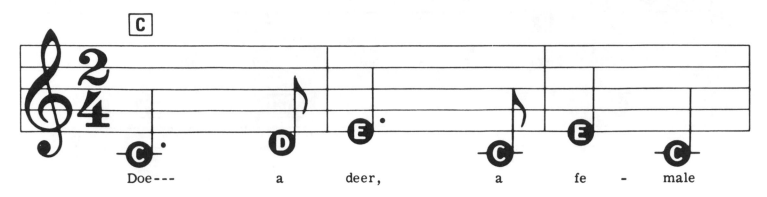

Doe--- a deer, a fe - male

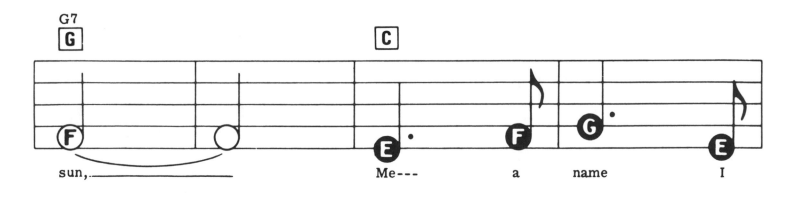

deer, Ray--- a drop of gold - en

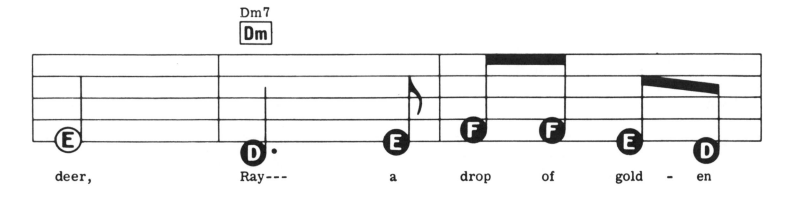

sun,_____ Me--- a name I

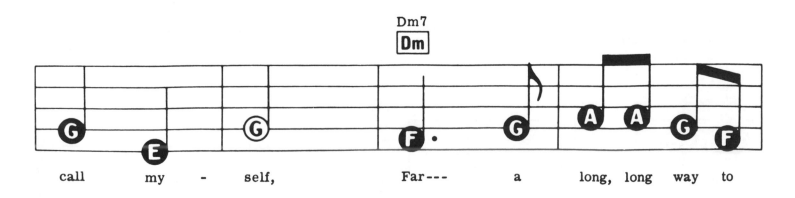

call my - self, Far--- a long, long way to

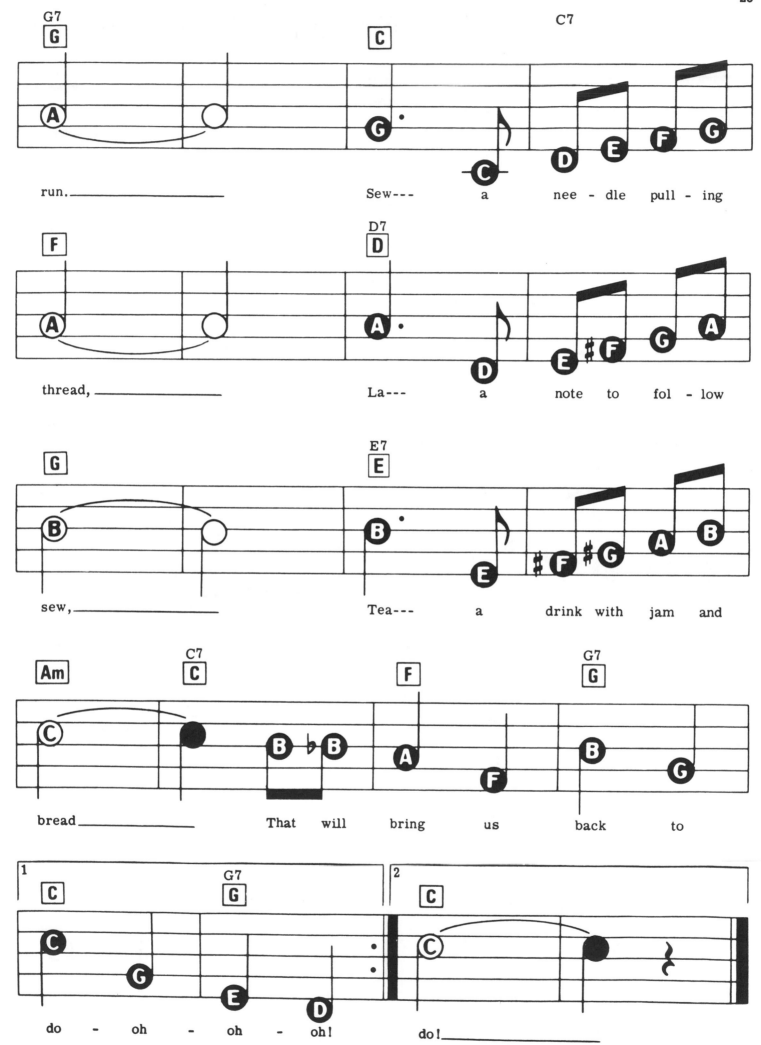

Don't Rain on My Parade
from *FUNNY GIRL*

Registration 4
Rhythm: Fox Trot

Words by Bob Merrill
Music by Jule Styne

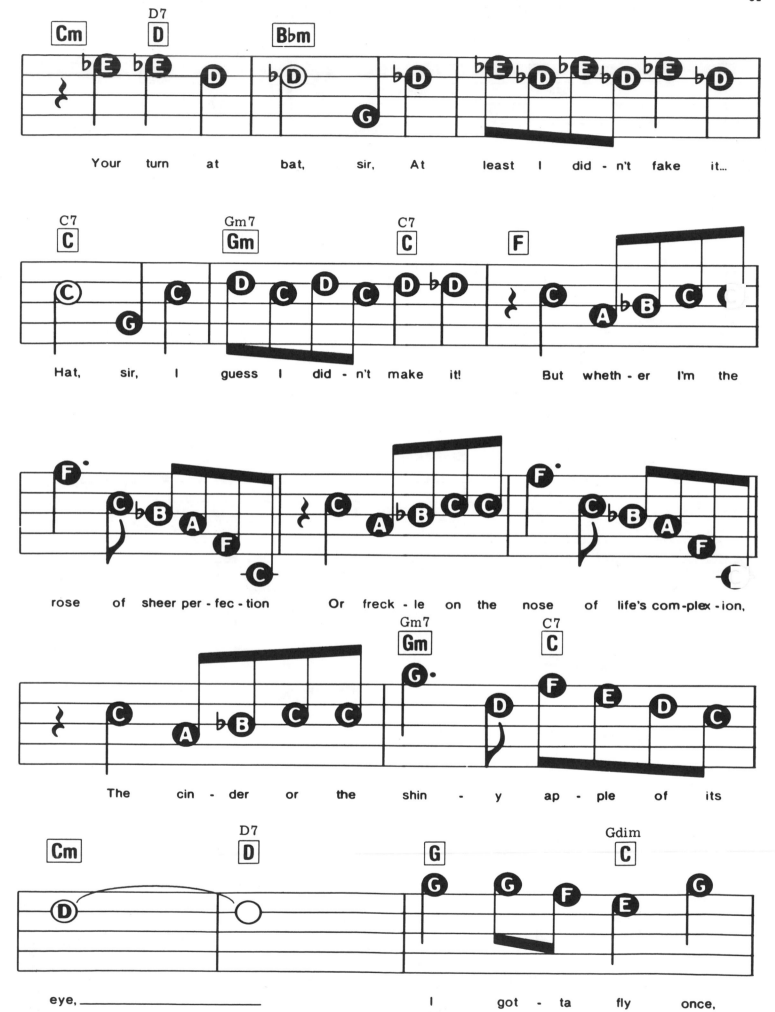

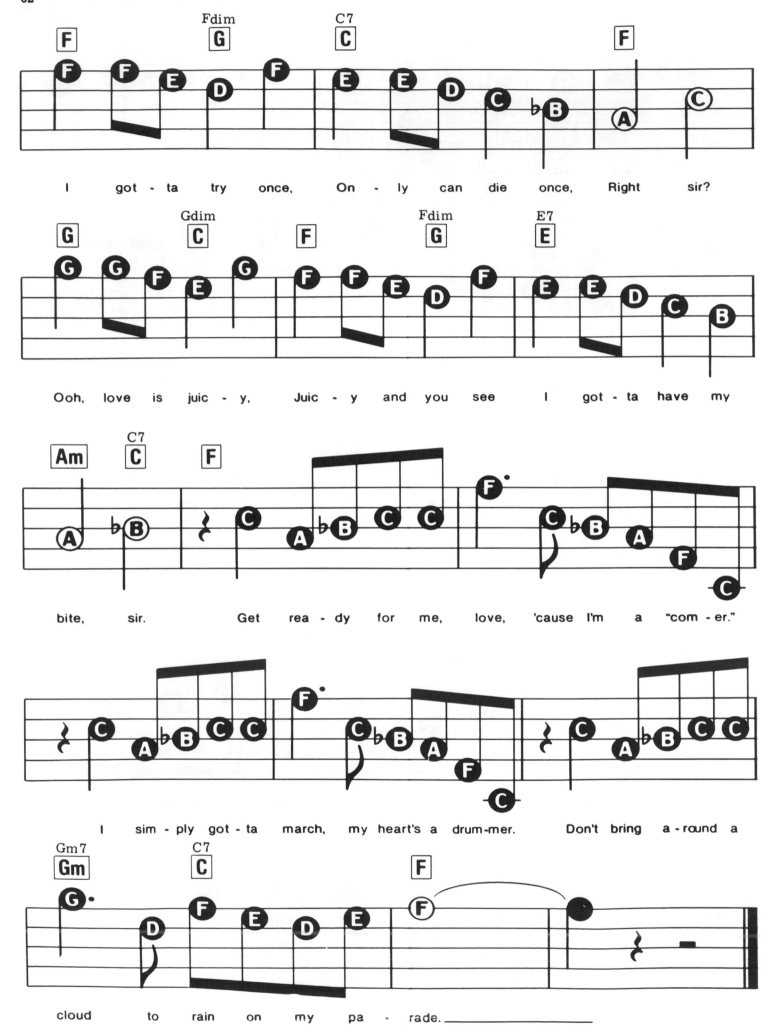

Get Me to the Church on Time

from MY FAIR LADY

Registration 3
Rhythm: Polka or Fox Trot

Words by Alan Jay Lerner
Music by Frederick Loewe

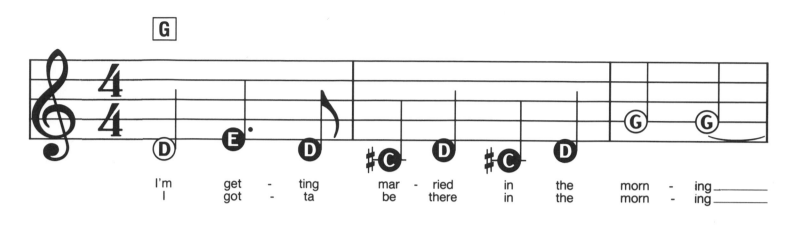

I'm get-ting mar-ried in the morn-ing ___
I got-ta be there in the morn-ing ___

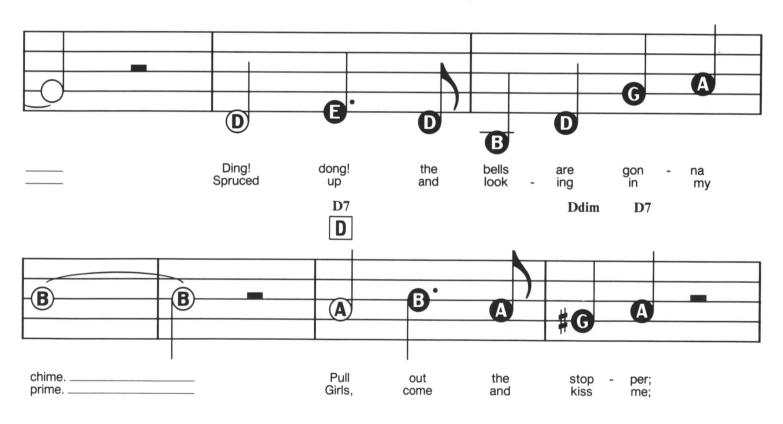

Ding! dong! the bells are gon-na
Spruced up and look-ing in my

chime. ___
prime. ___

Pull out the stop-per;
Girls, come and kiss me;

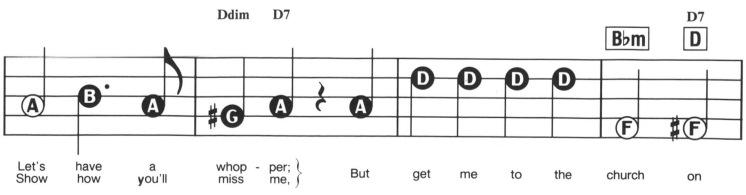

Let's have a whop-per; But get me to the church on
Show how you'll miss me,

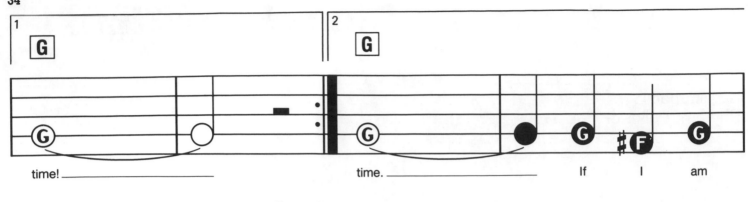

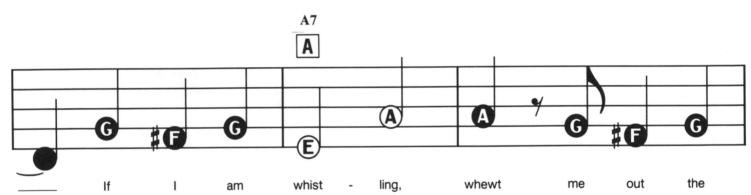

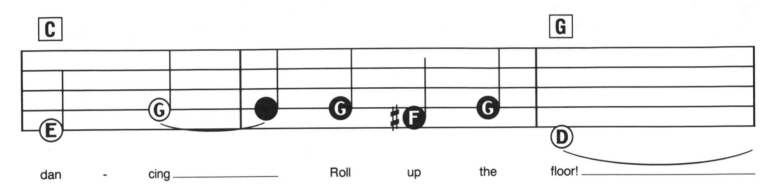

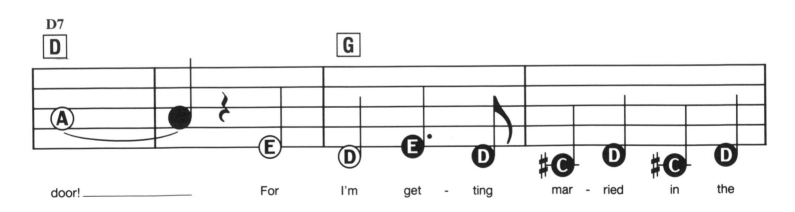

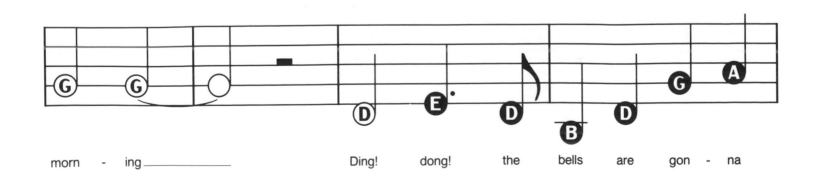

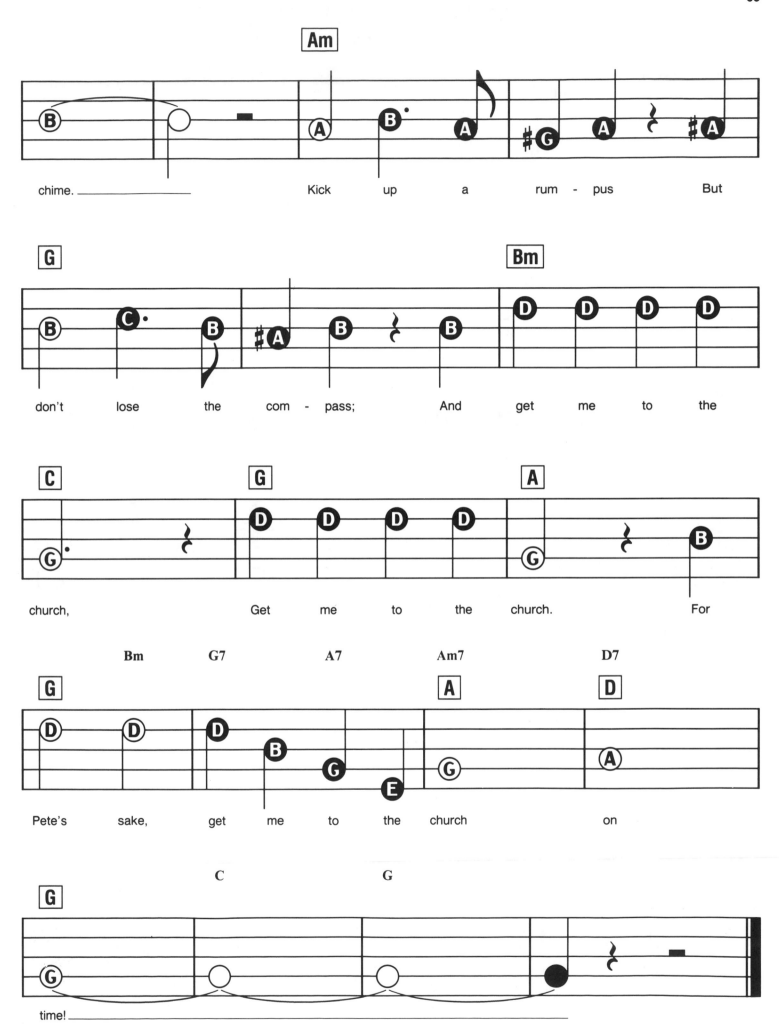

Easter Parade
from AS THOUSANDS CHEER

Registration 5
Rhythm: Fox Trot or Ballad

Words and Music by
Irving Berlin

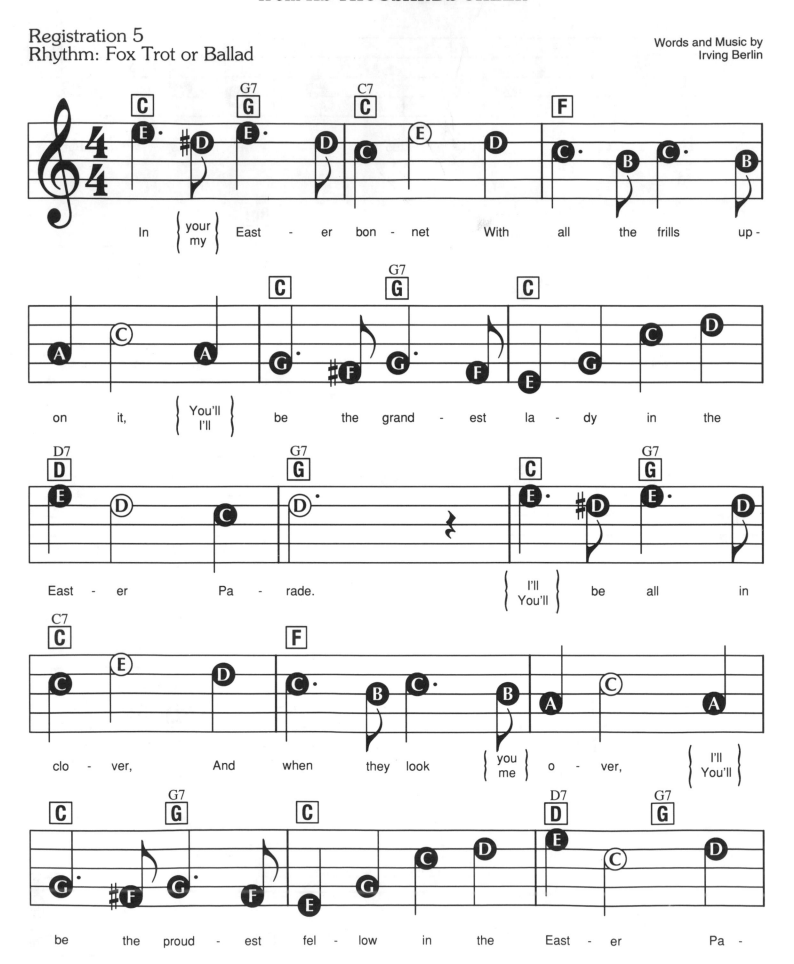

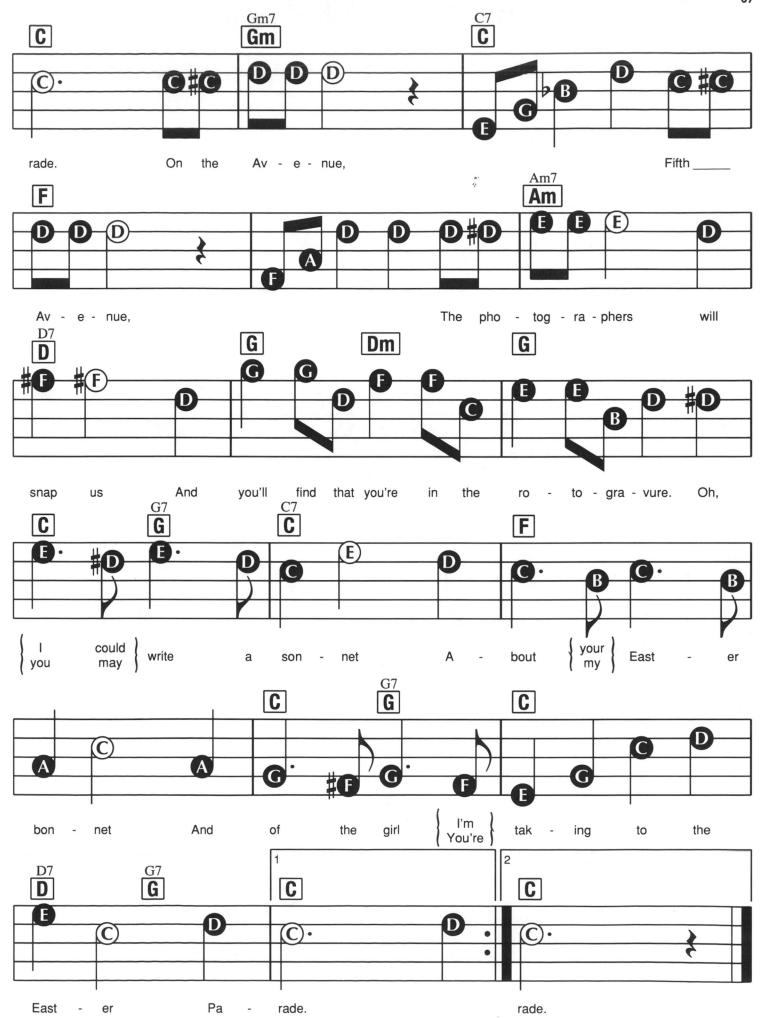

Glad to Be Unhappy
from ON YOUR TOES

Registration 3
Rhythm: Swing

Words by Lorenz Hart
Music by Richard Rodgers

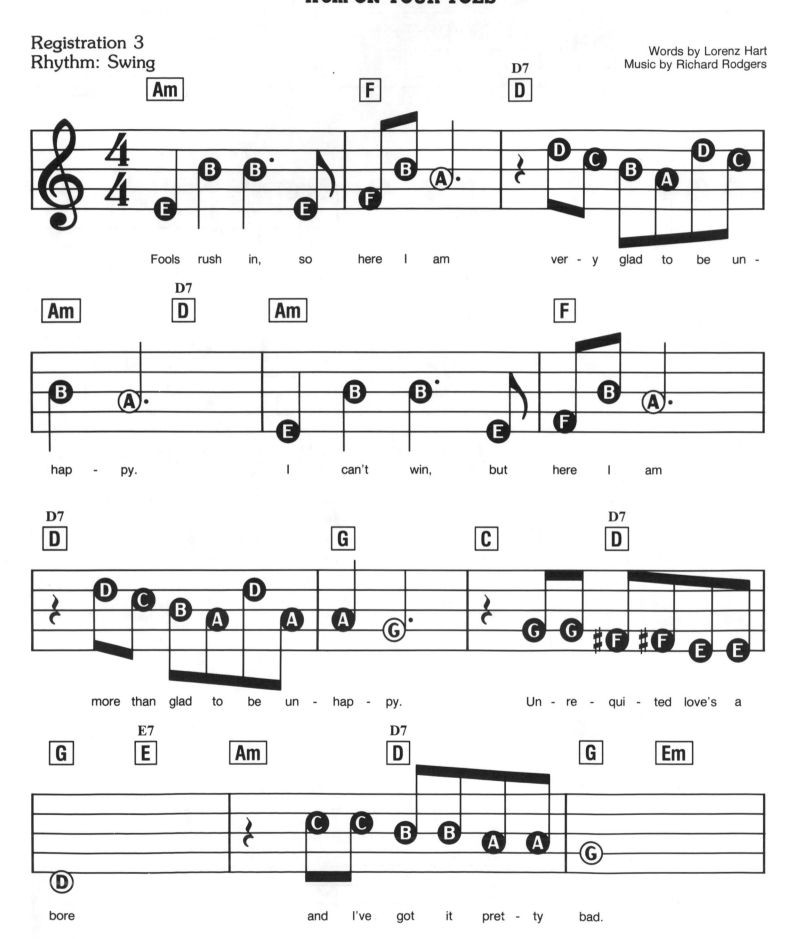

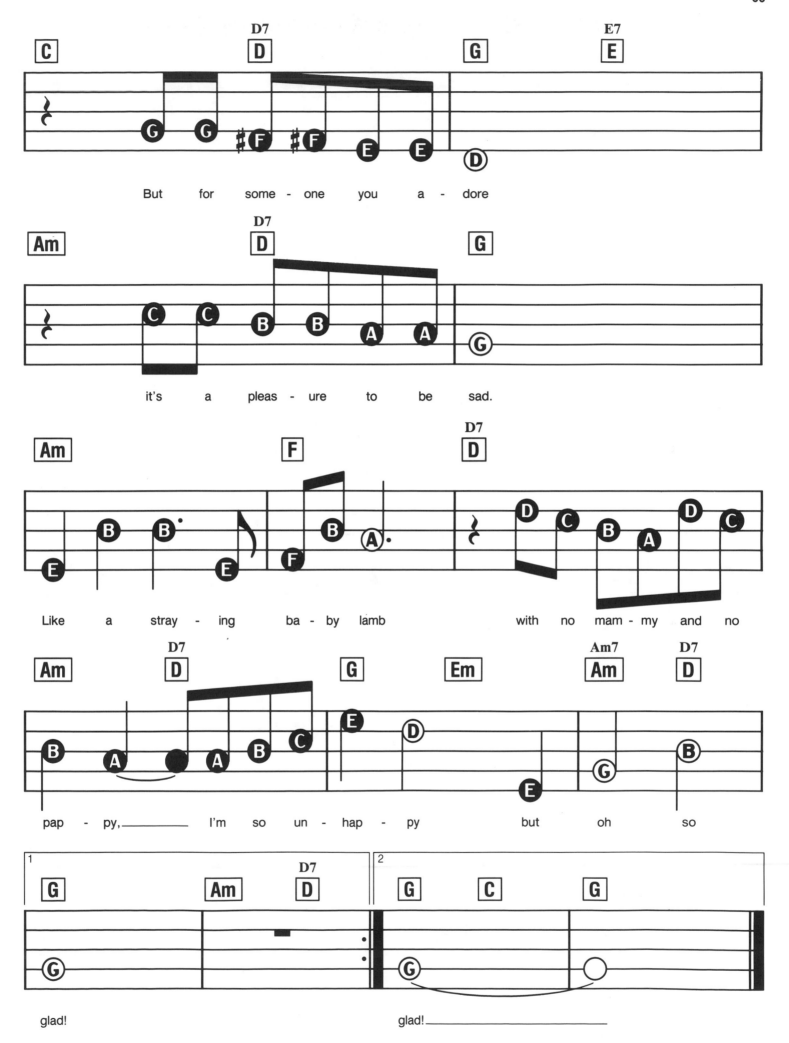

Goodnight, My Someone

from Meredith Willson's THE MUSIC MAN

Registration 10
Rhythm: Waltz

By Meredith Willson

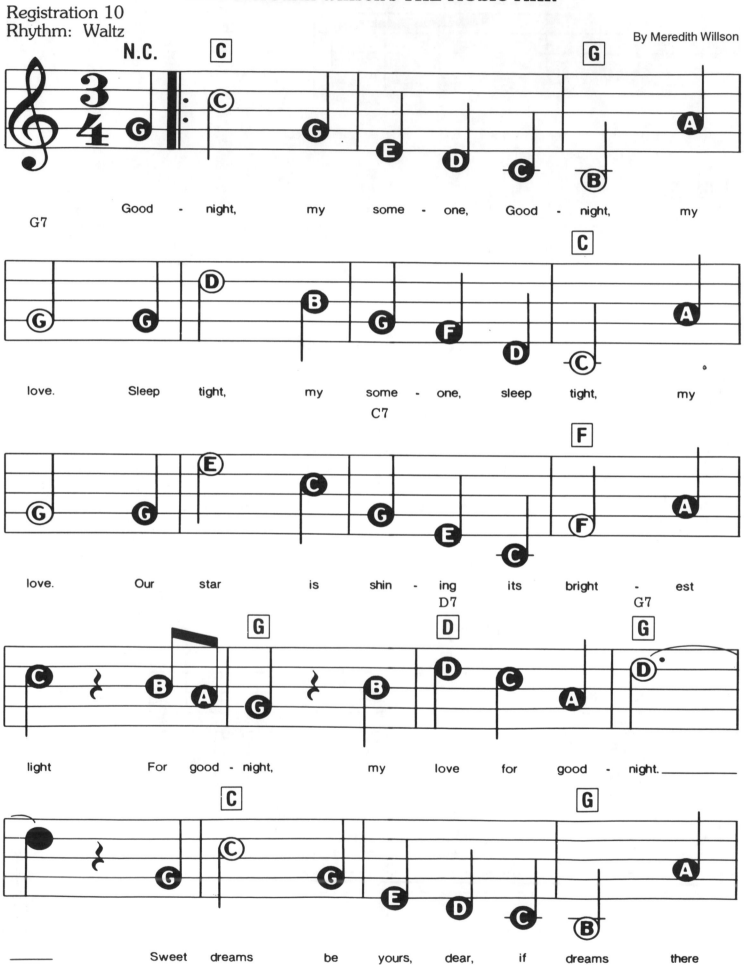

Good - night, my some - one, Good - night, my love. Sleep tight, my some - one, sleep tight, my love. Our star is shin - ing its bright - est light For good - night, my love for good - night. _____ _____ Sweet dreams be yours, dear, if dreams there

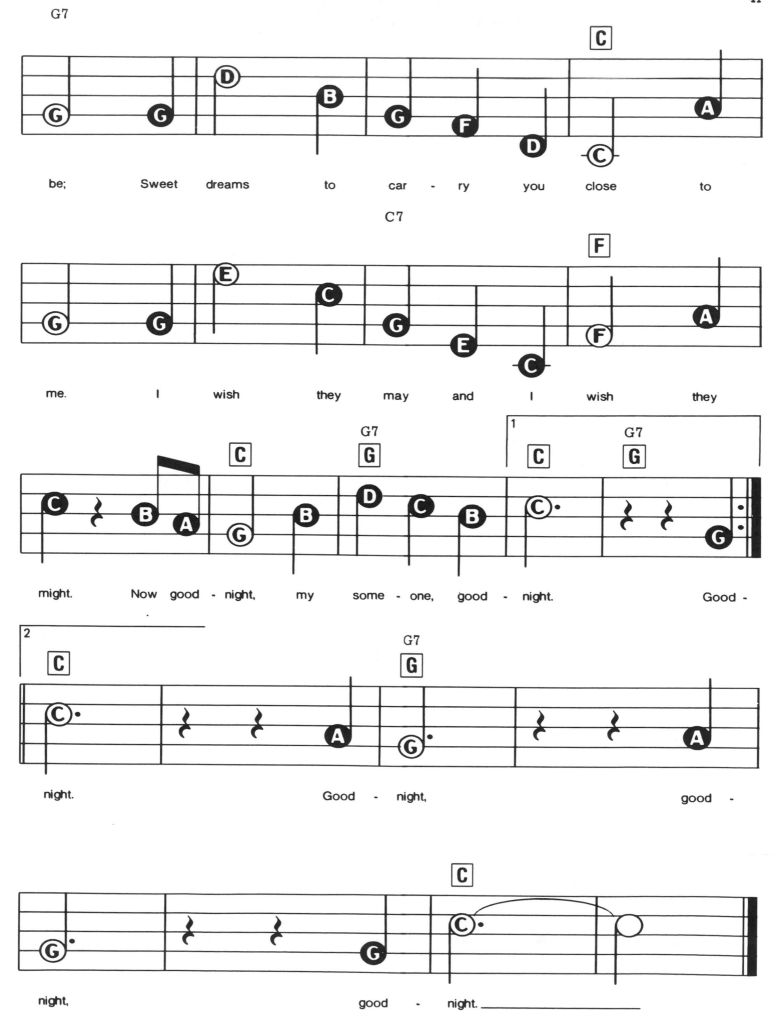

be; Sweet dreams to car - ry you close to

me. I wish they may and I wish they

might. Now good - night, my some - one, good - night. Good -

night. Good - night,

good -

night, good - night. _____

Hello, Dolly!

from HELLO, DOLLY!

Registration 5
Rhythm: Swing

Music and Lyric by
Jerry Herman

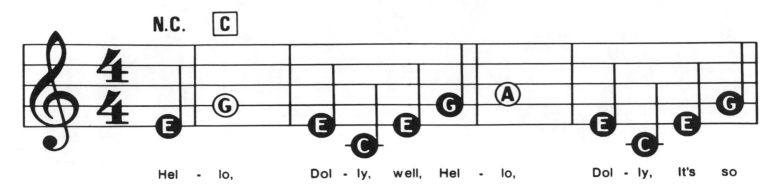

Hel - lo, Dol - ly, well, Hel - lo, Dol - ly, It's so

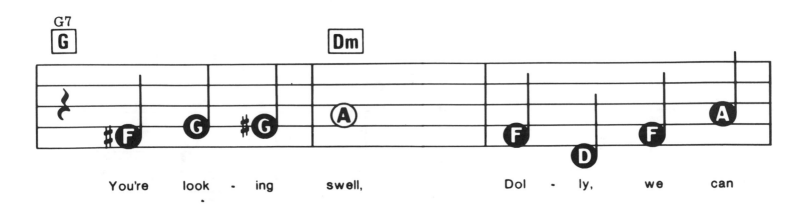

nice to have you back where you be - long.

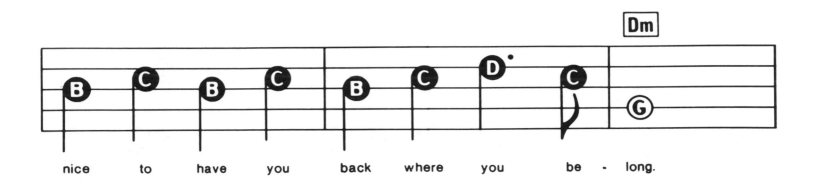

You're look - ing swell, Dol - ly, we can

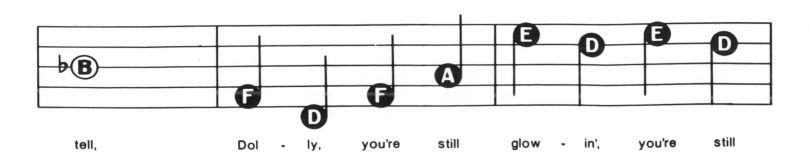

tell, Dol - ly, you're still glow - in', you're still

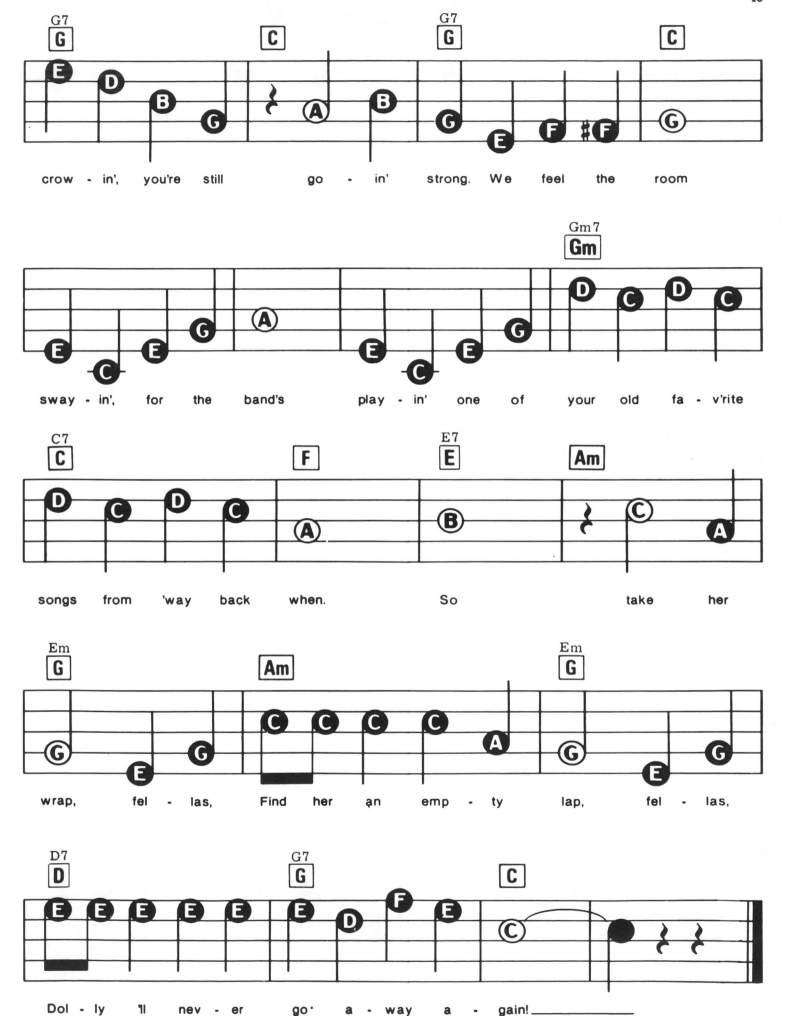

I Ain't Down Yet
from THE UNSINKABLE MOLLY BROWN

Registration 4
Rhythm: Polka, March or Fox Trot

By Meredith Willson

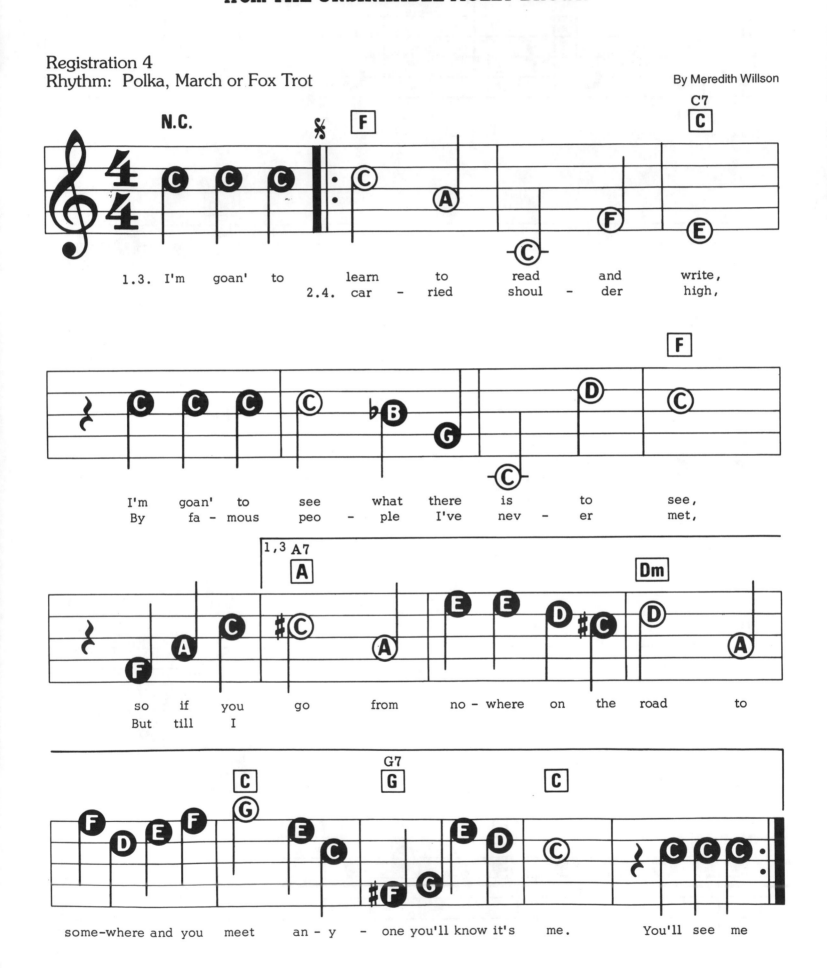

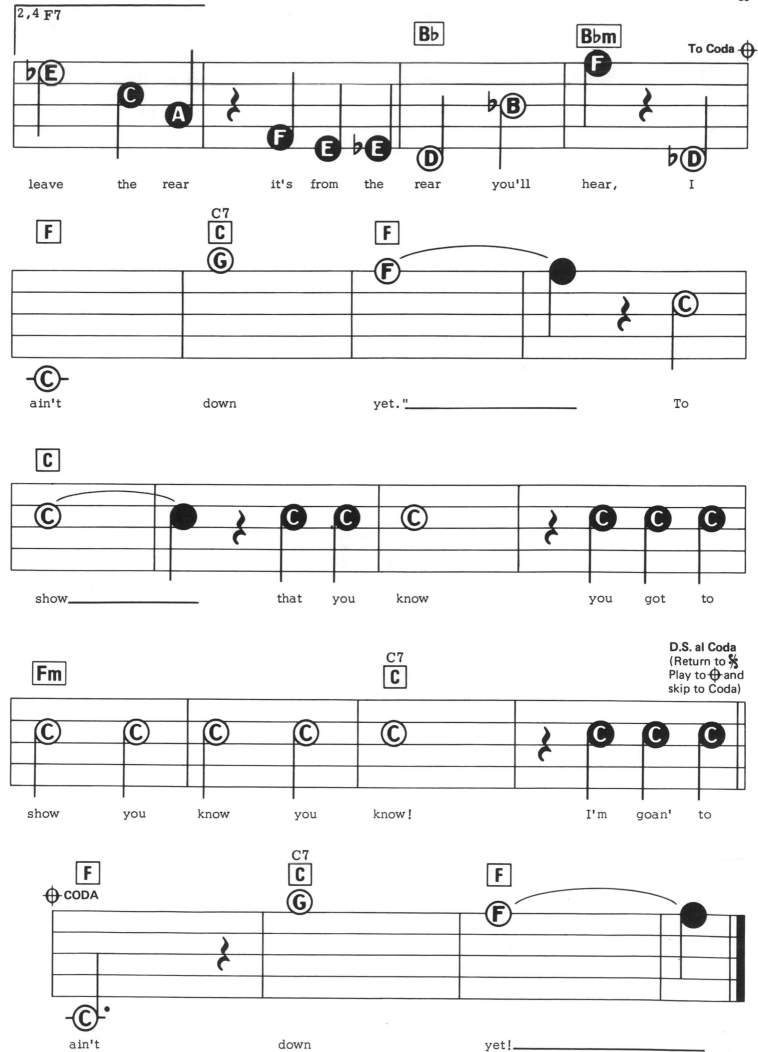

I Dreamed a Dream
from LES MISÉRABLES

Music by Claude-Michel Schönberg
Lyrics by Herbert Kretzmer
Original Text by Alain Boublil and Jean-Marc Natel

Registration 1
Rhythm: Fox Trot or Ballad

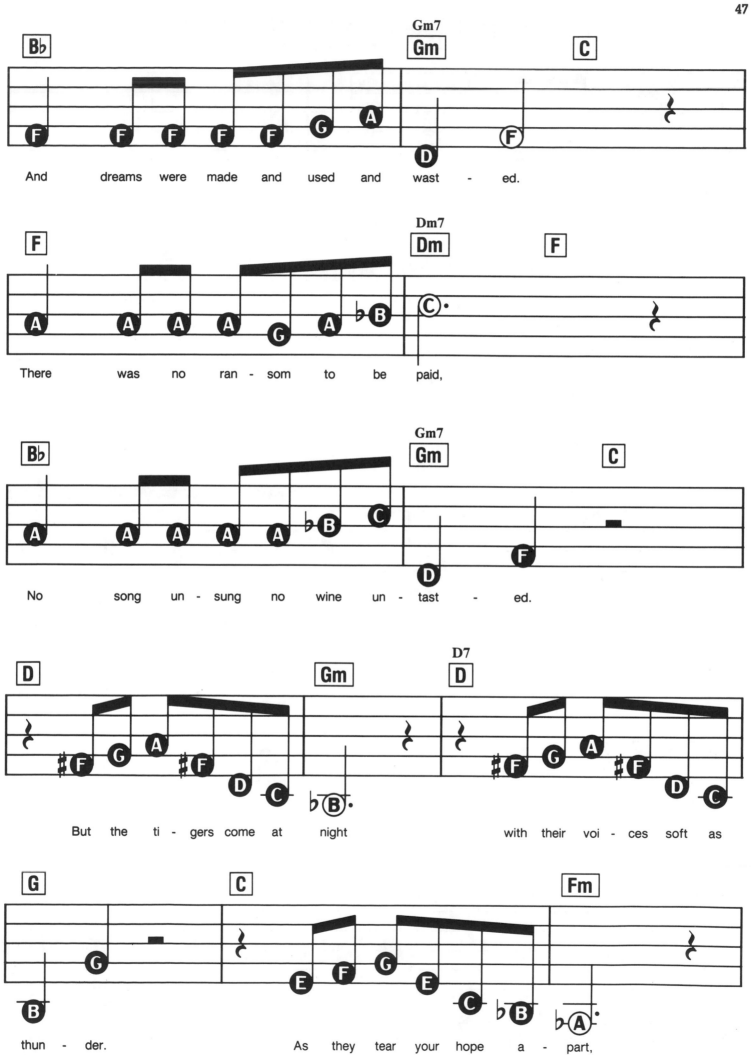

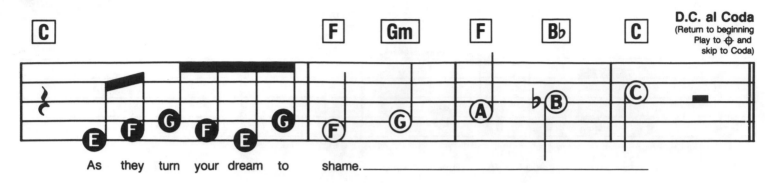

D.C. al Coda
(Return to beginning
Play to ⊕ and
skip to Coda)

As they turn your dream to shame.____

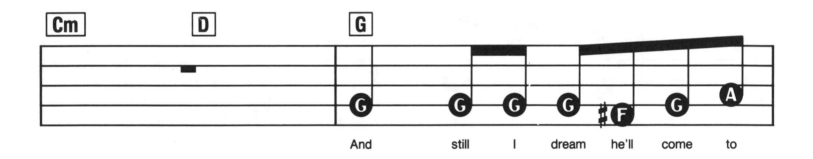

But he was gone when au-tumn came.

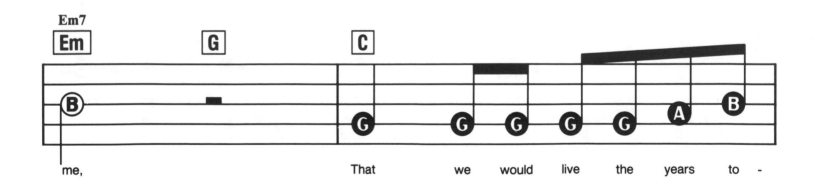

And still I dream he'll come to

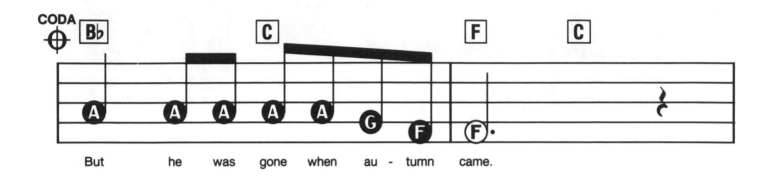

me, That we would live the years to -

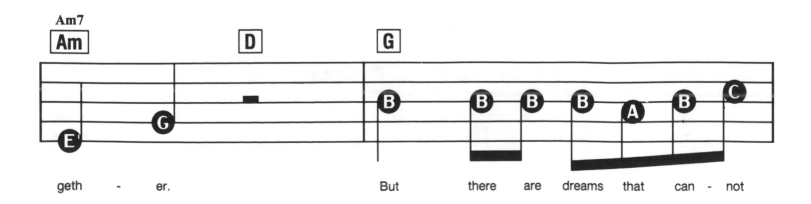

geth - er. But there are dreams that can - not

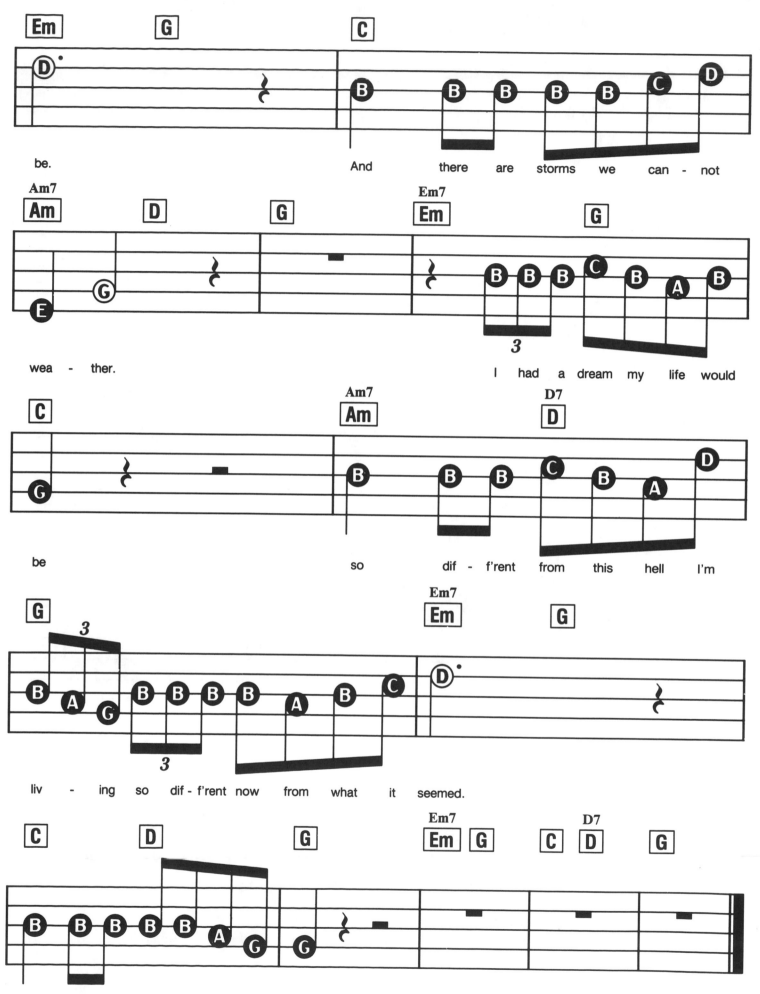

be.

And there are storms we can - not

wea - ther.

I had a dream my life would

be

so dif - f'rent from this hell I'm

liv - ing so dif - f'rent now from what it seemed.

Now life has killed the dream I dreamed.

I Enjoy Being a Girl
from FLOWER DRUM SONG

Registration 2
Rhythm: Fox Trot, Polka or Pops

Lyrics by Oscar Hammerstein II
Music by Richard Rodgers

When I have a brand new hair - do ____
men say I'm cute and fun - ny ____

With my eye - lash - es all in curl, ____
And my teeth are - n't all teeth but pearl, ____

I float as the clouds on air do, ____
I just lap it up like hon - ey. ____

I en - joy be - ing a
I en - joy be - ing a

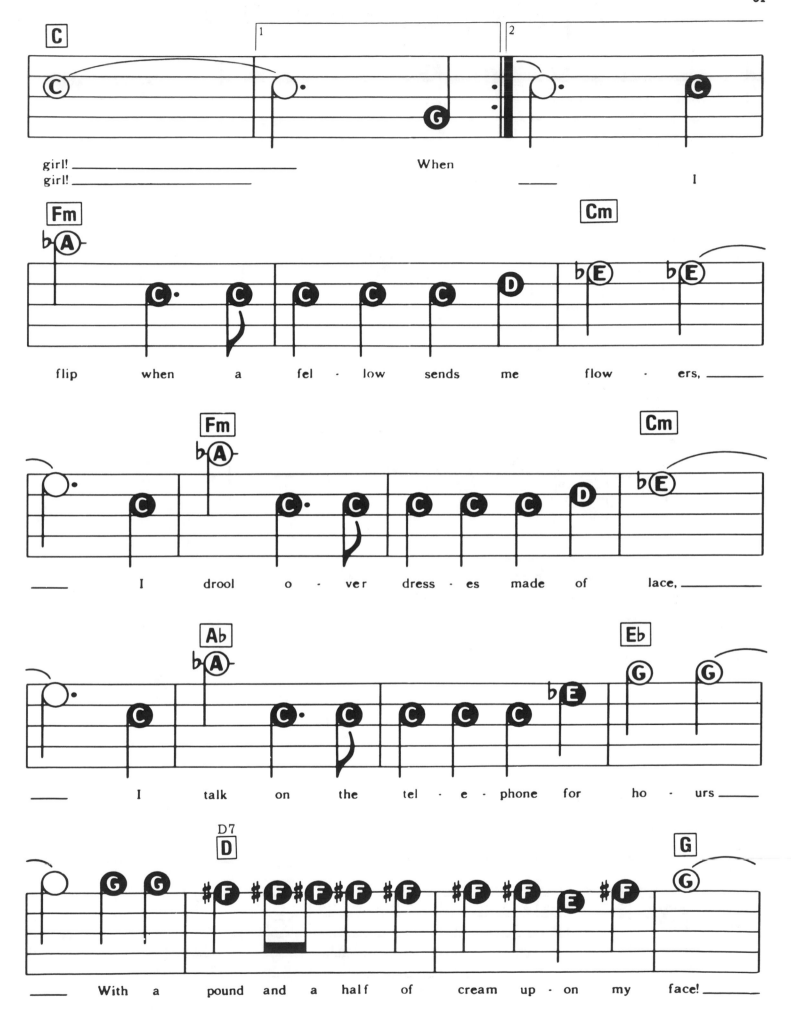

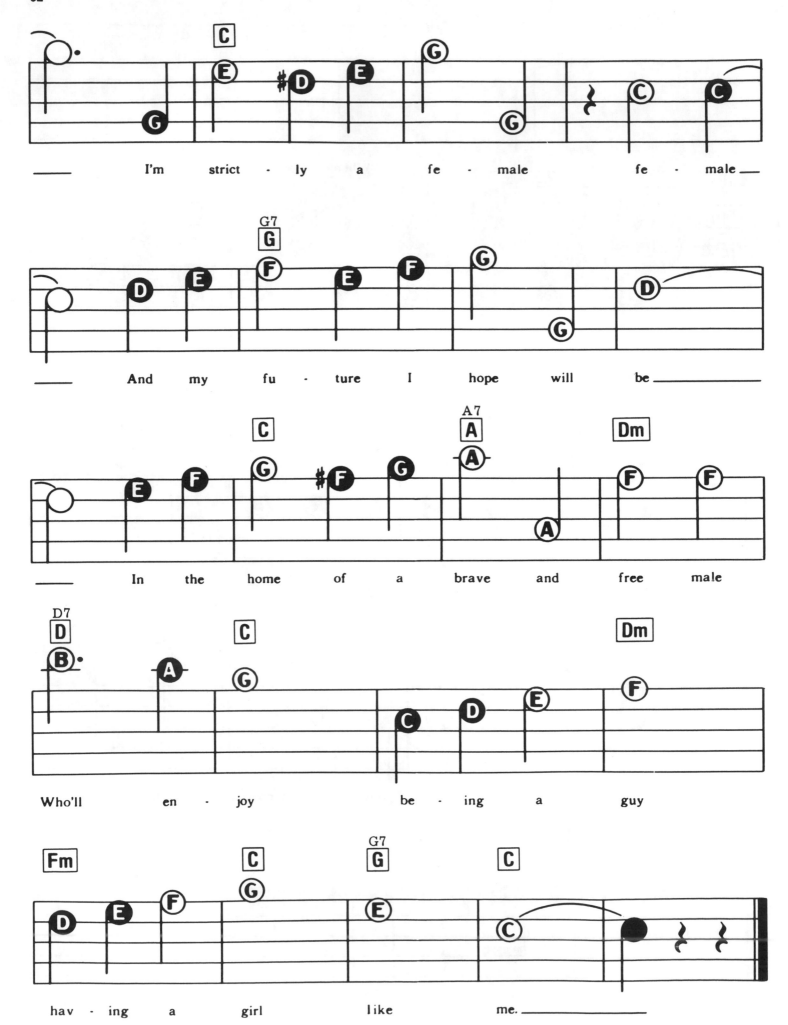

I Got the Sun in the Morning
from the Stage Production ANNIE GET YOUR GUN

Registration 7
Rhythm: Swing

Words and Music by
Irving Berlin

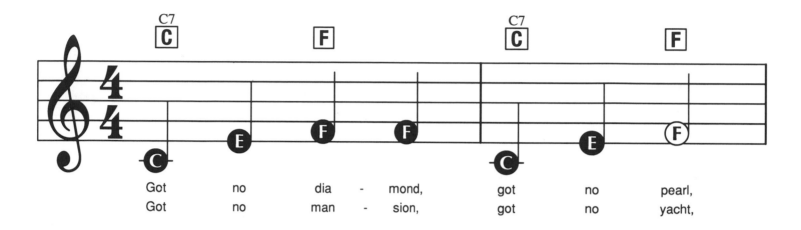

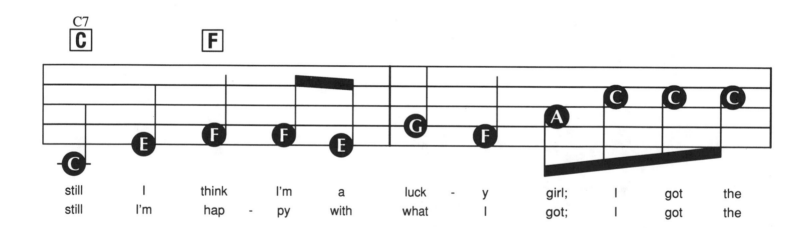

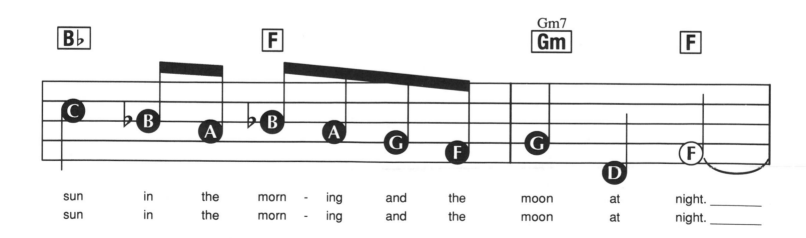

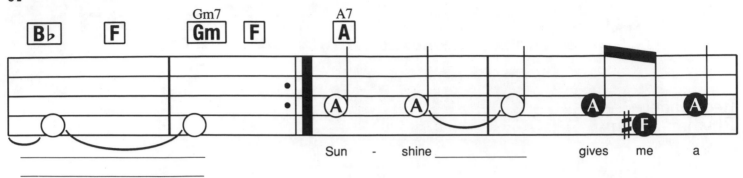

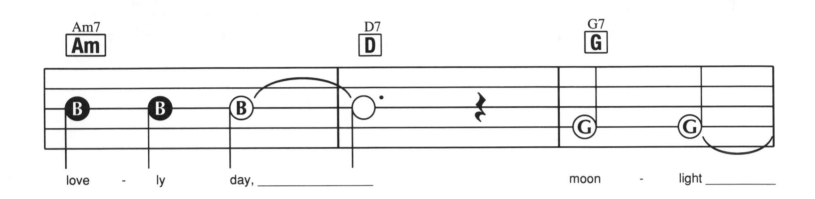

Sun - shine _____ gives me a

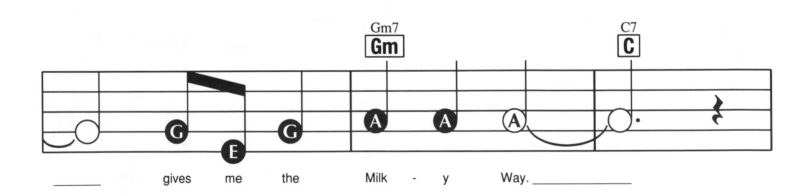

love - ly day, _____ moon - light _____

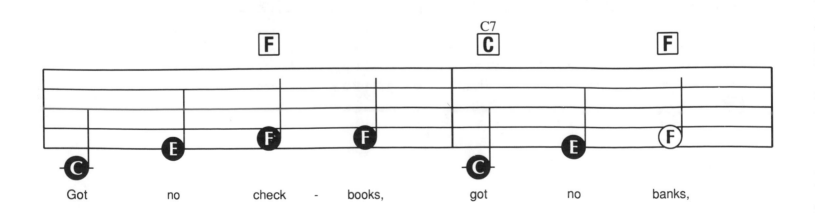

_____ gives me the Milk - y Way. _____

Got no check - books, got no banks,

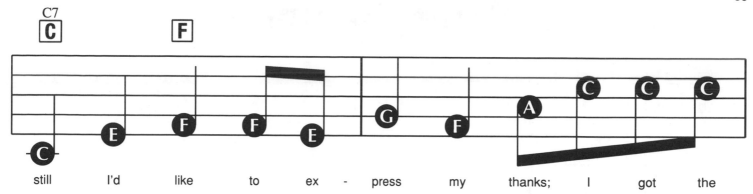

still I'd like to ex - press my thanks; I got the

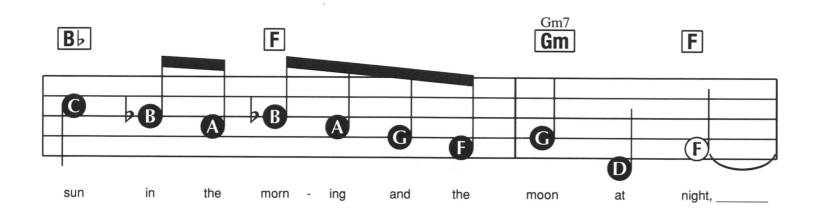

sun in the morn - ing and the moon at night, _____

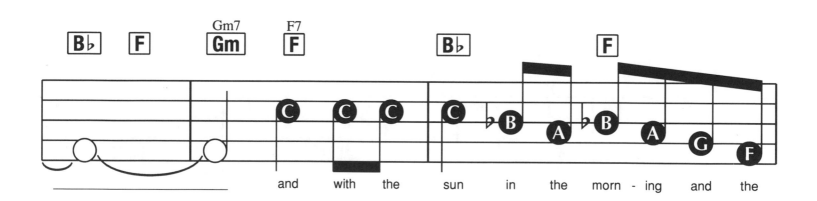

_____ and with the sun in the morn - ing and the

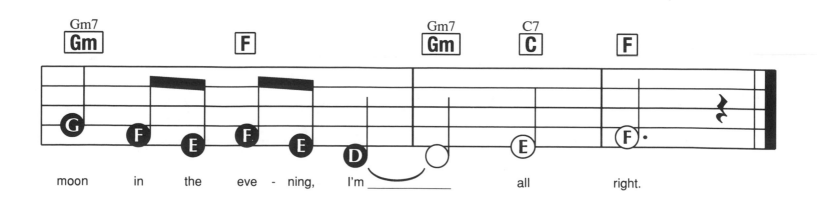

moon in the eve - ning, I'm _____ all right.

I Have Dreamed
from THE KING AND I

Registration 2
Rhythm: Swing

Lyrics by Oscar Hammerstein II
Music by Richard Rodgers

I have dreamed _____ that your arms are love - ly _____

I have dreamed _____ what a joy you'll be _____

I have dreamed _____ ev - 'ry word you'll whis - per _____ When you're

close, _____ close to me. _____

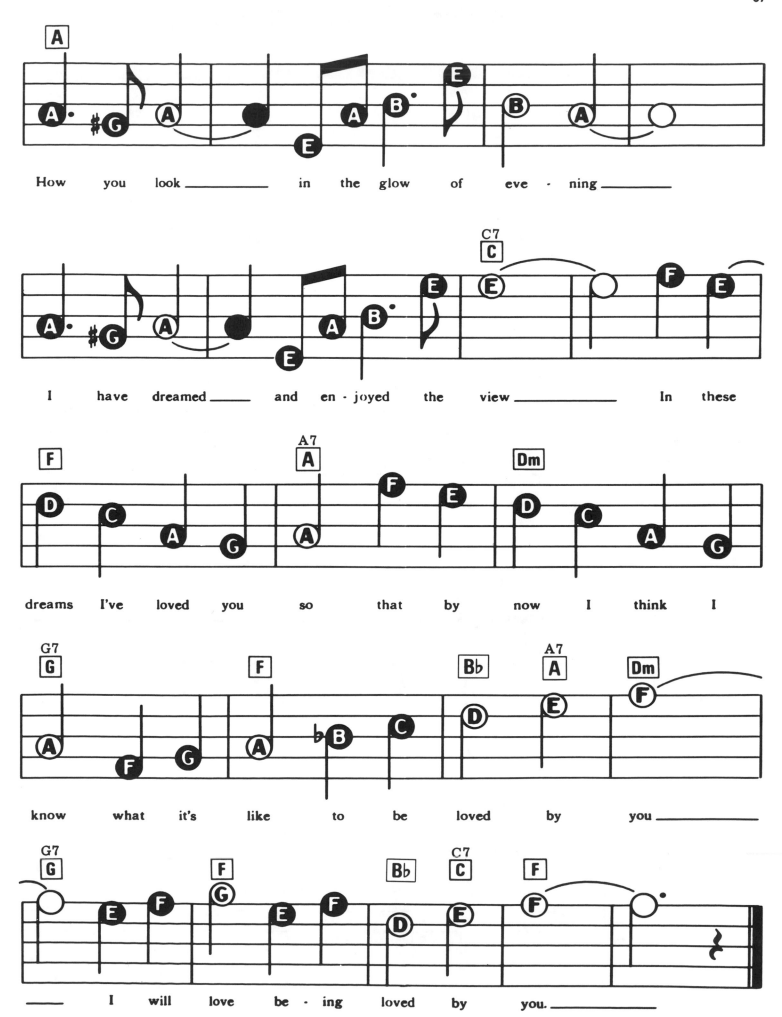

I Wish I Were in Love Again
from BABES IN ARMS

Registration 7
Rhythm: Swing

Words by Lorenz Hart
Music by Richard Rodgers

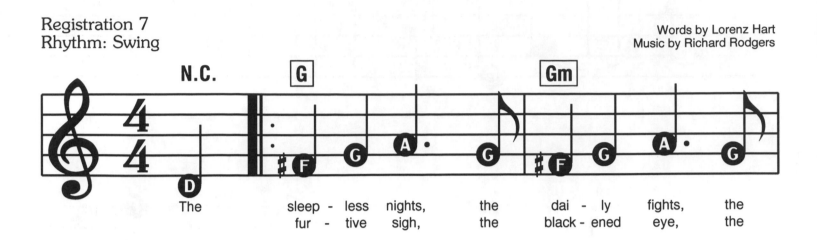

The sleep - less nights, the dai - ly fights, the
fur - tive sigh, the black - ened eye, the

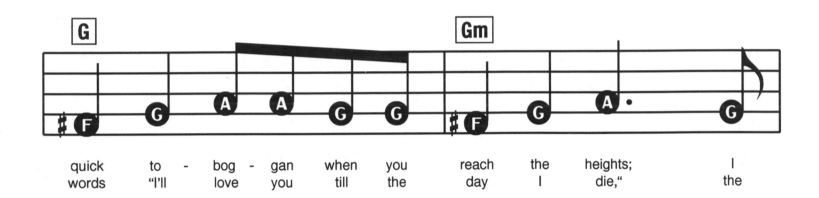

quick to - bog - gan when you reach the heights; I
words "I'll love you till the day I die," the

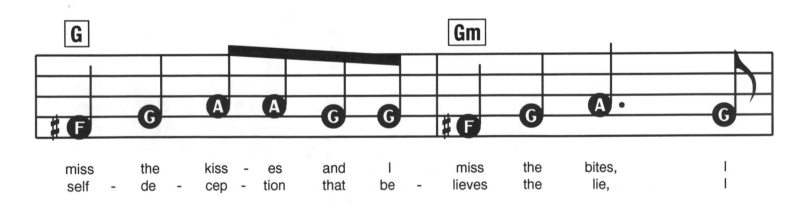

miss the kiss - es and I miss the bites, I
self - de - cep - tion that be - lieves the lie, I

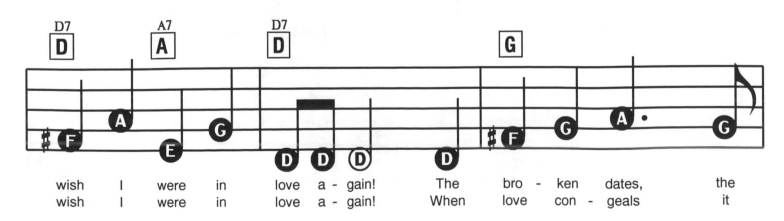

wish I were in love a - gain! The bro - ken dates, the
wish I were in love a - gain! When love con - geals it

59

The Impossible Dream
(The Quest)
from MAN OF LA MANCHA

Registration 3
Rhythm: Waltz

Lyric by Joe Darion
Music by Mitch Leigh

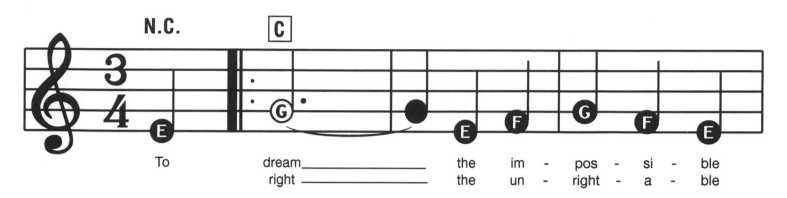

To dream_____ the im - pos - si - ble
right _____ the un - right - a - ble

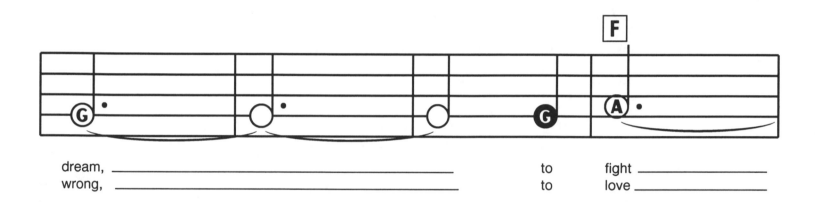

dream, _____ to fight _____
wrong, _____ to love _____

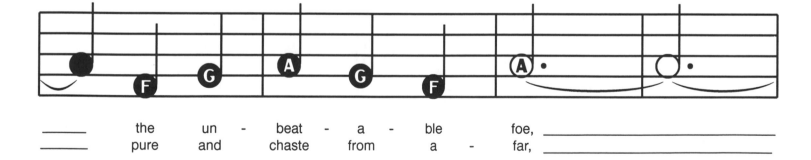

_____ the un - beat - a - ble foe, _____
_____ pure and chaste from a - far, _____

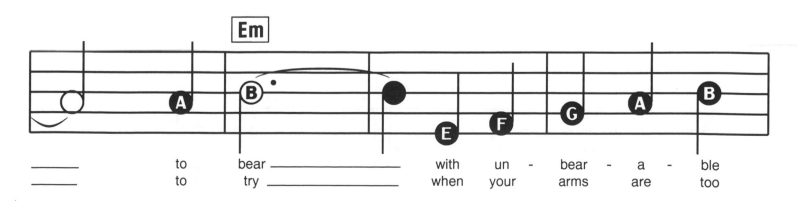

_____ to bear _____ with un - bear - a - ble
_____ to try _____ when your arms are too

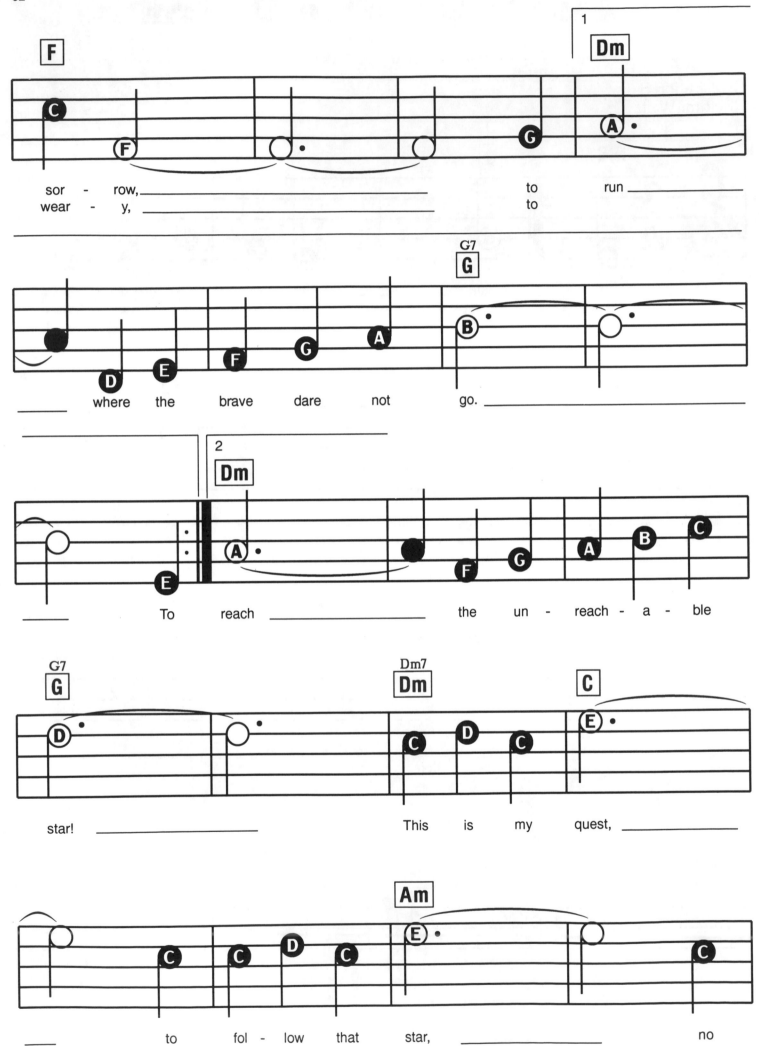

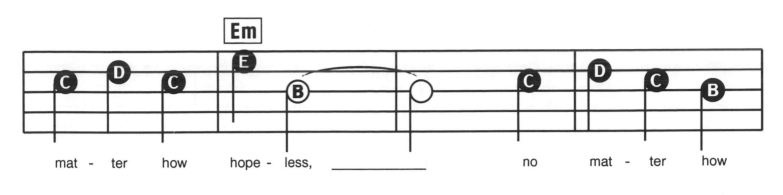

mat - ter how hope - less, _____ no mat - ter how

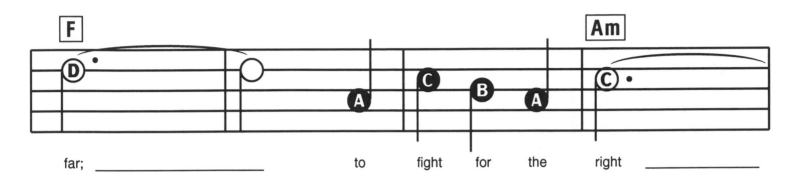

far; _____ to fight for the right _____

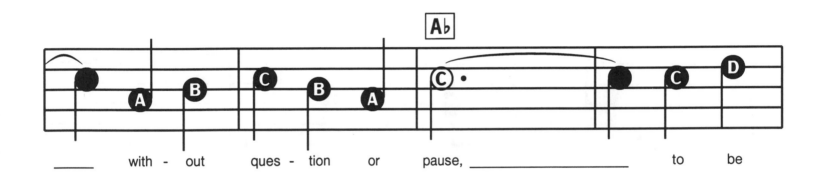

_____ with - out ques - tion or pause, _____ to be

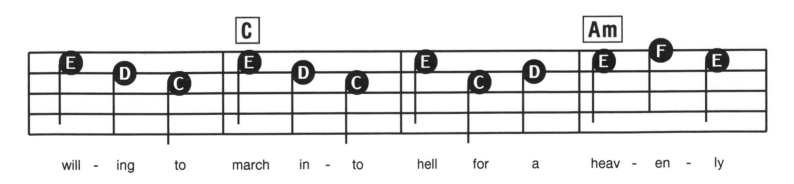

will - ing to march in - to hell for a heav - en - ly

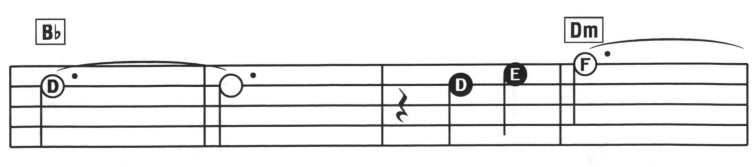

cause! _____ And I know, _____

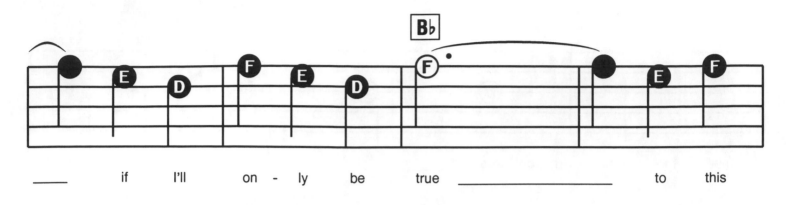

if I'll on - ly be true _____ to this

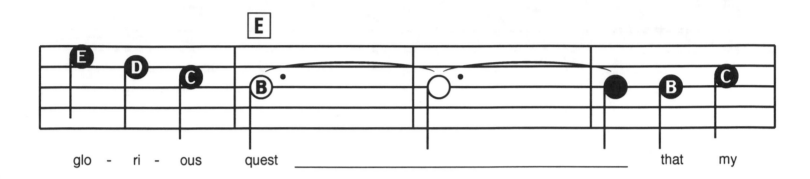

glo - ri - ous quest _____ that my

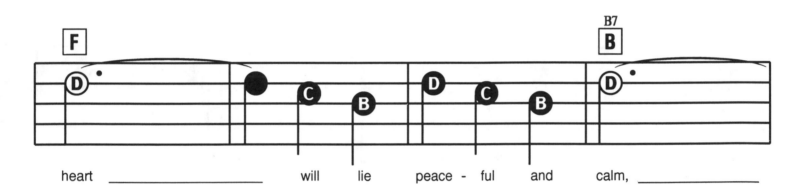

heart _____ will lie peace - ful and calm, _____

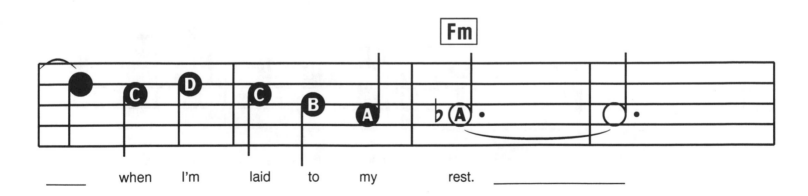

when I'm laid to my rest. _____

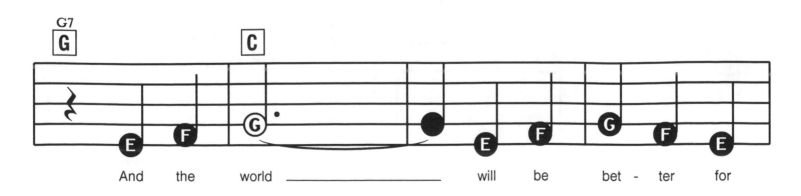

And the world _____ will be bet - ter for

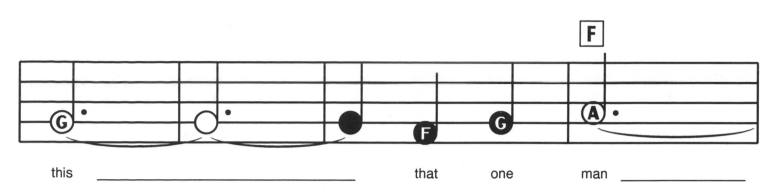

this _____ that one man _____

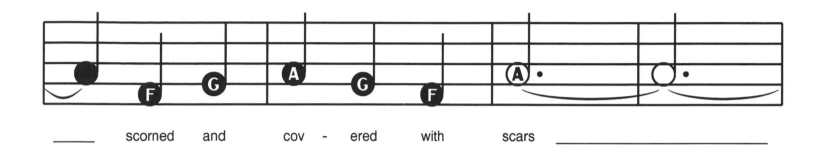

___ scorned and cov - ered with scars _____

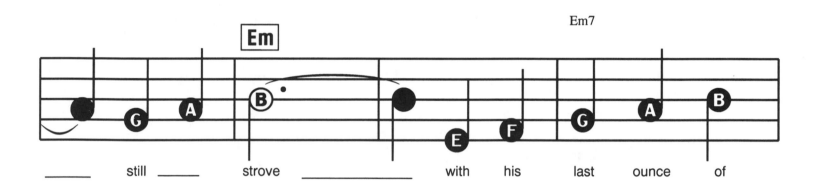

___ still ___ strove _____ with his last ounce of

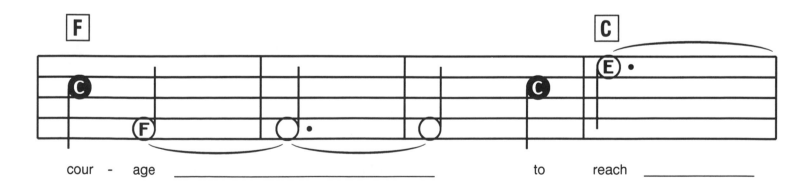

cour - age _____ to reach _____

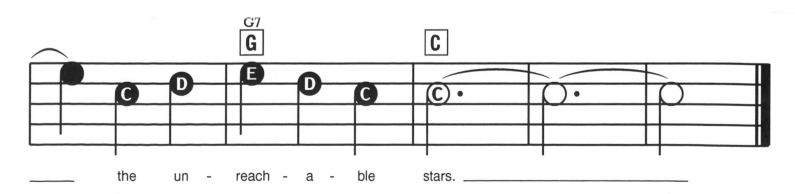

___ the un - reach - a - ble stars. _____

I'd Do Anything
from the Broadway Musical OLIVER!

Registration 10
Rhythm: Ballad

Words and Music by
Lionel Bart

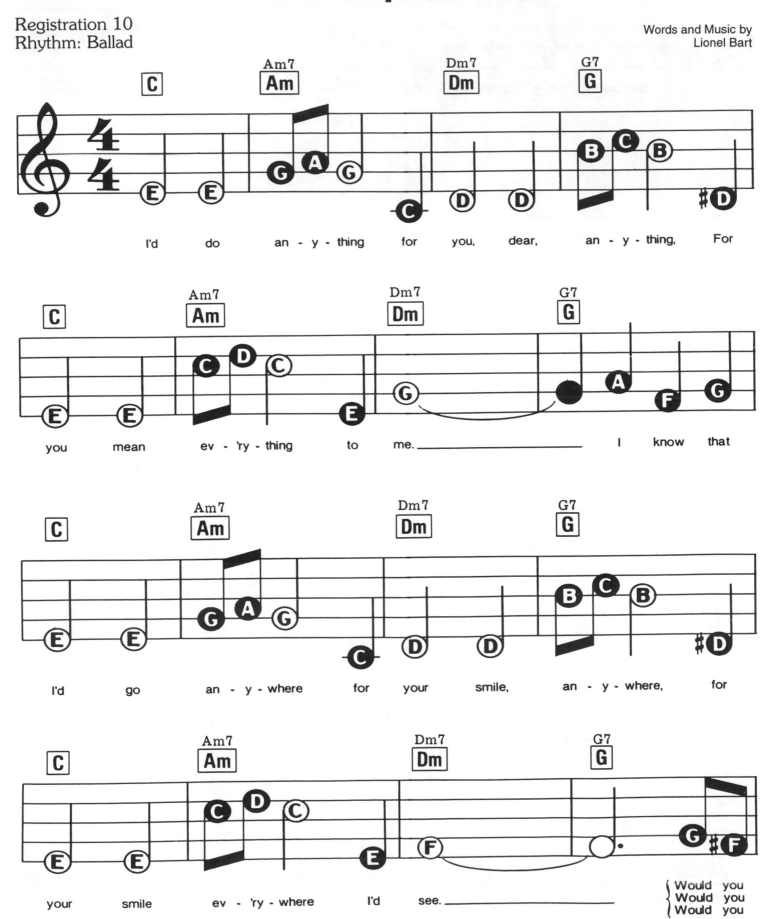

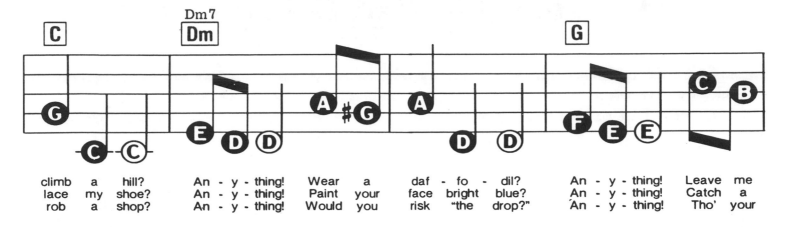

climb a hill? An - y - thing! Wear a daf - fo - dil? An - y - thing! Leave me
lace my shoe? An - y - thing! Paint your face bright blue? An - y - thing! Catch a
rob a shop? An - y - thing! Would you risk "the drop?" An - y - thing! Tho' your

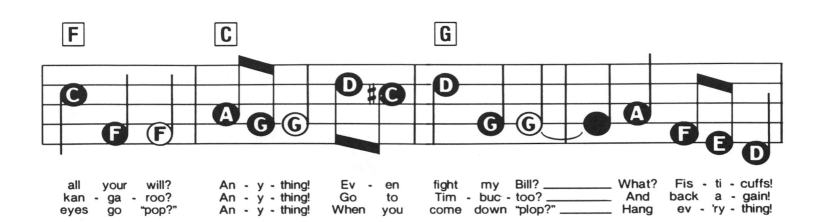

all your will? An - y - thing! Ev - en fight my Bill? _____ What? Fis - ti - cuffs!
kan - ga - roo? An - y - thing! Go to Tim - buc - too? _____ And back a - gain!
eyes go "pop?" An - y - thing! When you come down "plop?" _____ Hang ev - 'ry - thing!

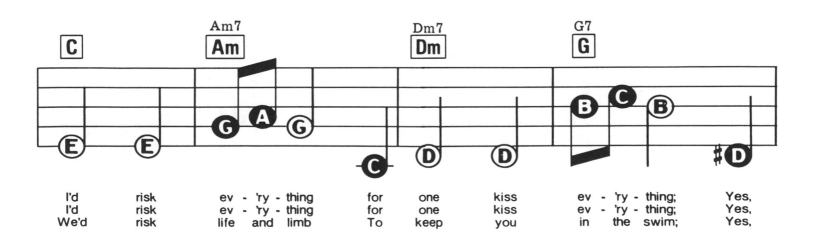

I'd risk ev - 'ry - thing for one kiss ev - 'ry - thing; Yes,
I'd risk ev - 'ry - thing for one kiss ev - 'ry - thing; Yes,
We'd risk life and limb To keep you in the swim; Yes,

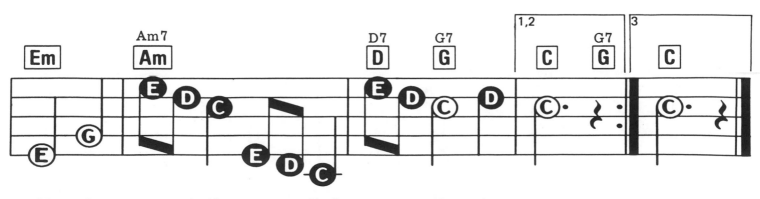

I'd do an - y - thing, an - y - thing? An - y - thing for you.
I'd do an - y - thing, an - y - thing? An - y - thing for you.
we'd do an - y - thing, an - y - thing? An - y - thing for you.

If Ever I Would Leave You

from CAMELOT

Registration 10
Rhythm: Fox Trot or Ballad

Words by Alan Jay Lerner
Music by Frederick Loewe

If ev-er I would leave you It would-n't be in
leave you It could-n't be in

sum - mer. See-ing you in sum - mer I
au - tumn. How I'd leave in au - tumn I

nev - er would go. Your hair streaked with
nev - er will know. I've seen how you

sun - light, Your lips red as flame,
spar - kle When fall nips the air.

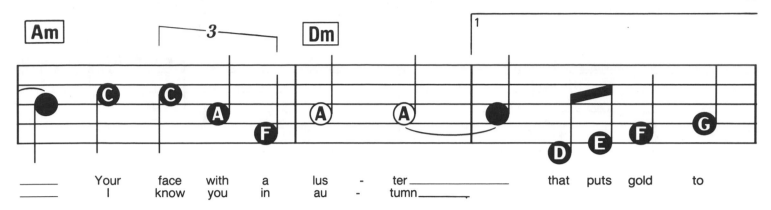

Your face with a lus - ter _____ that puts gold to
I know you in au - tumn _____

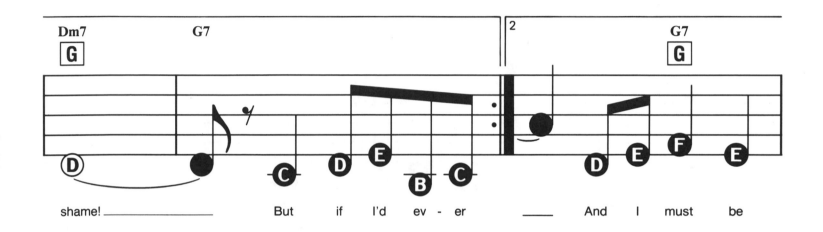

shame! _____ But if I'd ev - er ____ And I must be

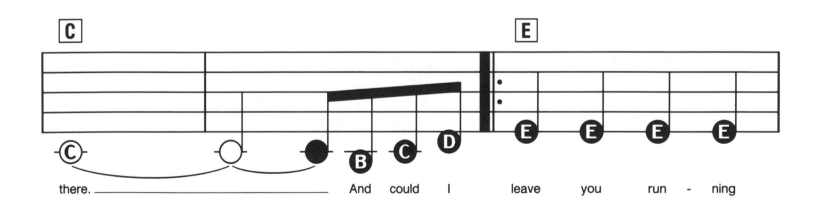

there. _____ And could I leave you run - ning

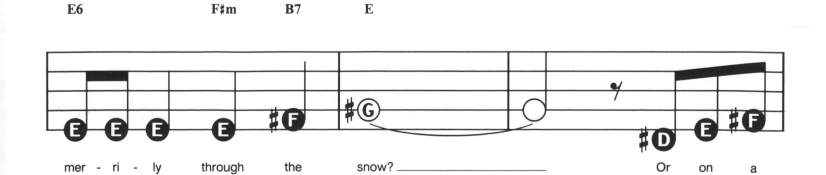

mer - ri - ly through the snow? _____ Or on a

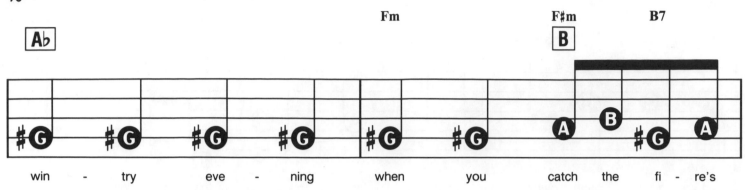

win - try eve - ning when you catch the fi - re's

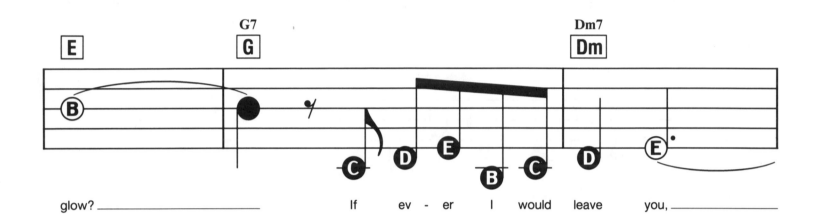

glow?   If ev - er I would leave you,

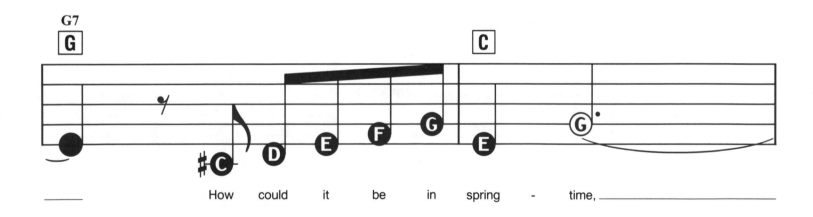

      How could it be in spring - time,

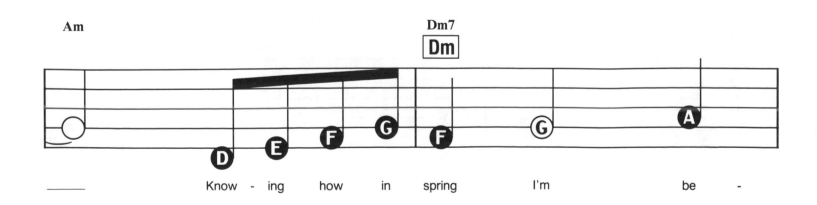

      Know - ing how in spring I'm be -

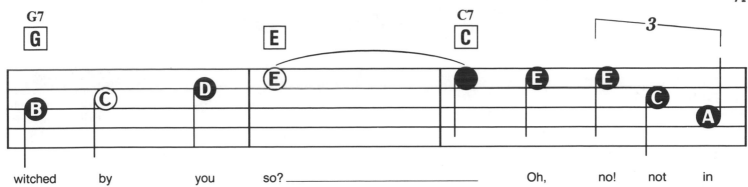

witched   by   you   so? _____   Oh,   no!   not   in

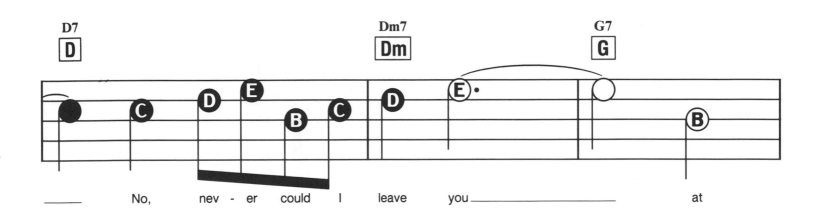

spring   -   time! _____   Sum - mer,   win - ter   or   fall! _____

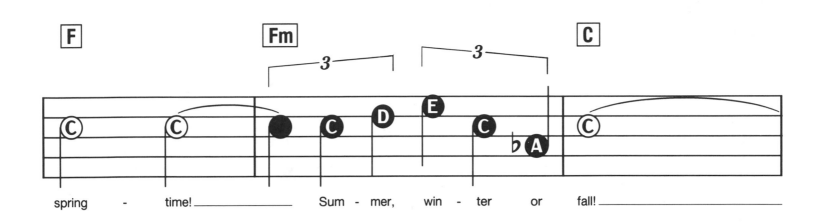

_____   No,   nev - er   could   I   leave   you _____   at

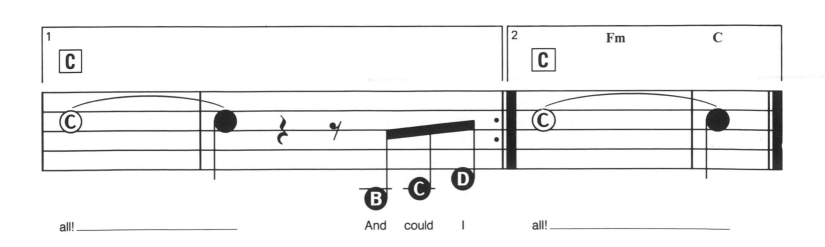

all! _____   And   could   I   all! _____

If I Loved You
from CAROUSEL

Registration 2
Rhythm: Ballad

Lyrics by Oscar Hammerstein II
Music by Richard Rodgers

If I loved you,
If I loved you,

Time and a-gain I would
Words would-n't come in an

try to say
eas - y way,

All
'Round

I'd
in

want
cir - cles

you
I'd

to

know.

go.

Long - in' to tell you, but a -

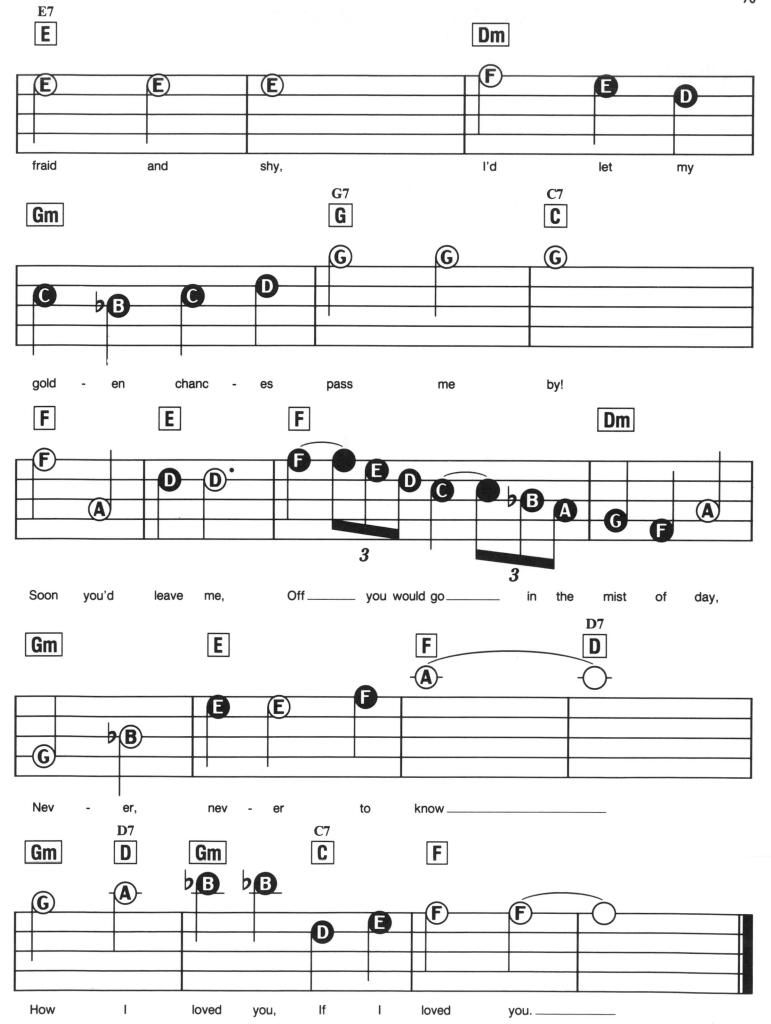

Losing My Mind
from FOLLIES

Registration 8
Rhythm: Broadway or 4/4 Ballad

Words and Music by
Stephen Sondheim

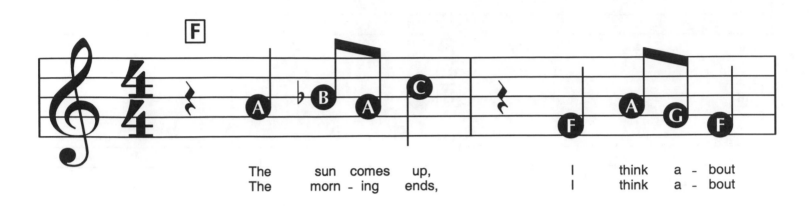

The sun comes up, I think a - bout
The morn - ing ends, I think a - bout

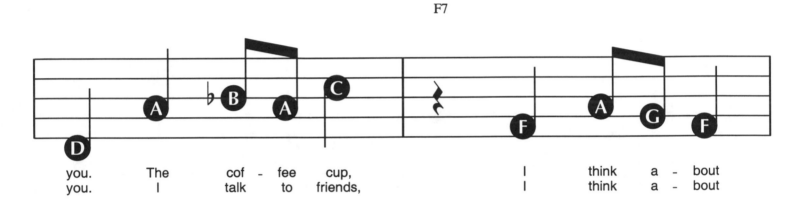

you. The cof - fee cup, I think a - bout
you. I talk to friends, I think a - bout

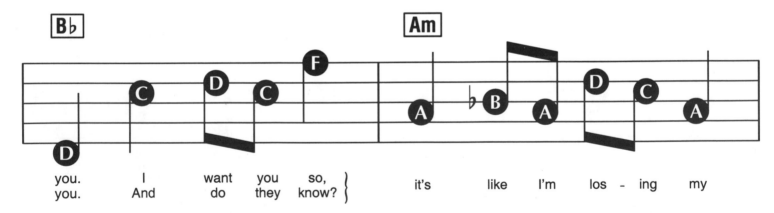

you. I want you so, } it's like I'm los - ing my
you. And do they know? }

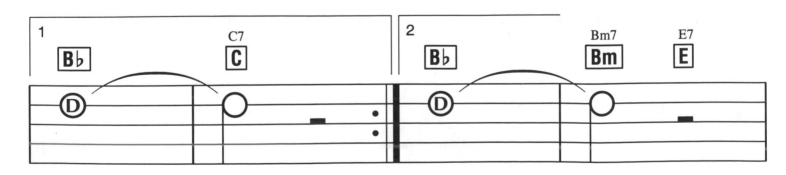

mind. _____ mind. _____

you. Spend sleep - less nights to think a - bout

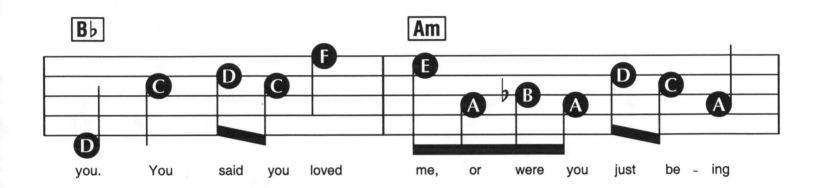

you. You said you loved me, or were you just be - ing

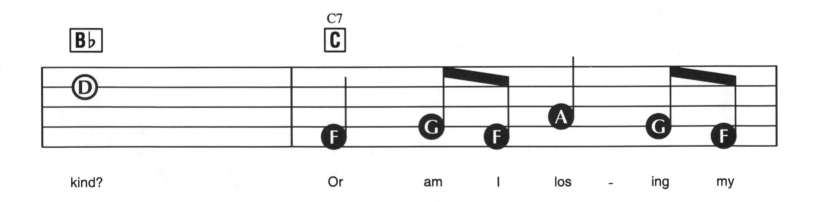

kind? Or am I los - ing my

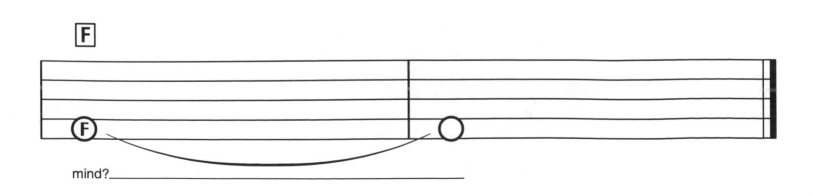

mind?

Lost in the Stars
from the Musical Production LOST IN THE STARS

Registration 9
Rhythm: Ballad

Words by Maxwell Anderson
Music by Kurt Weill

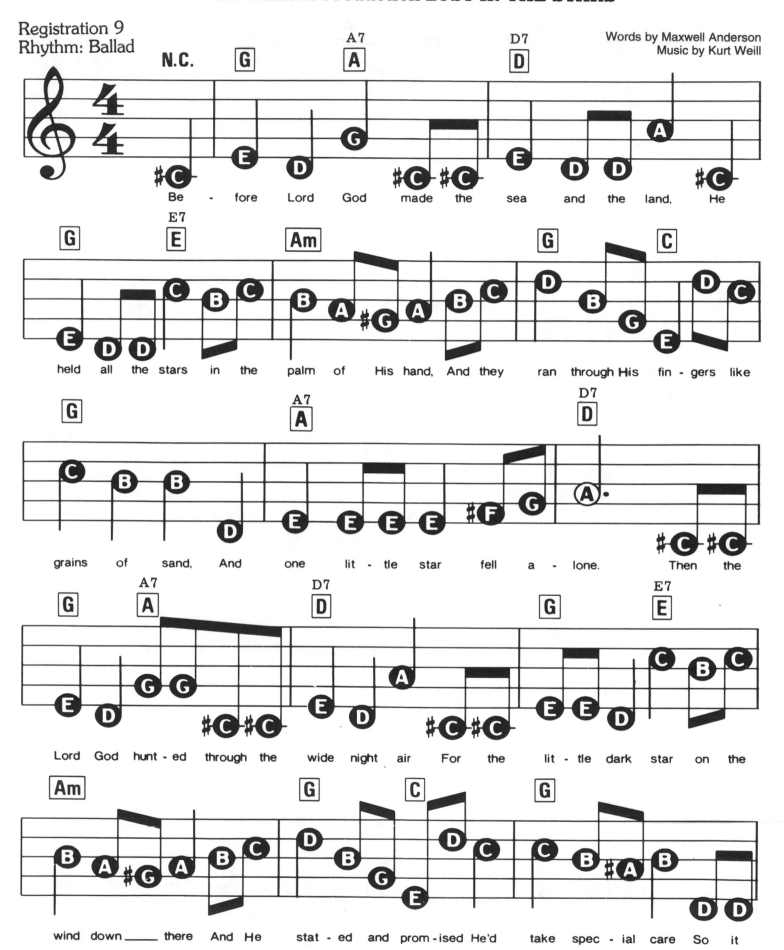

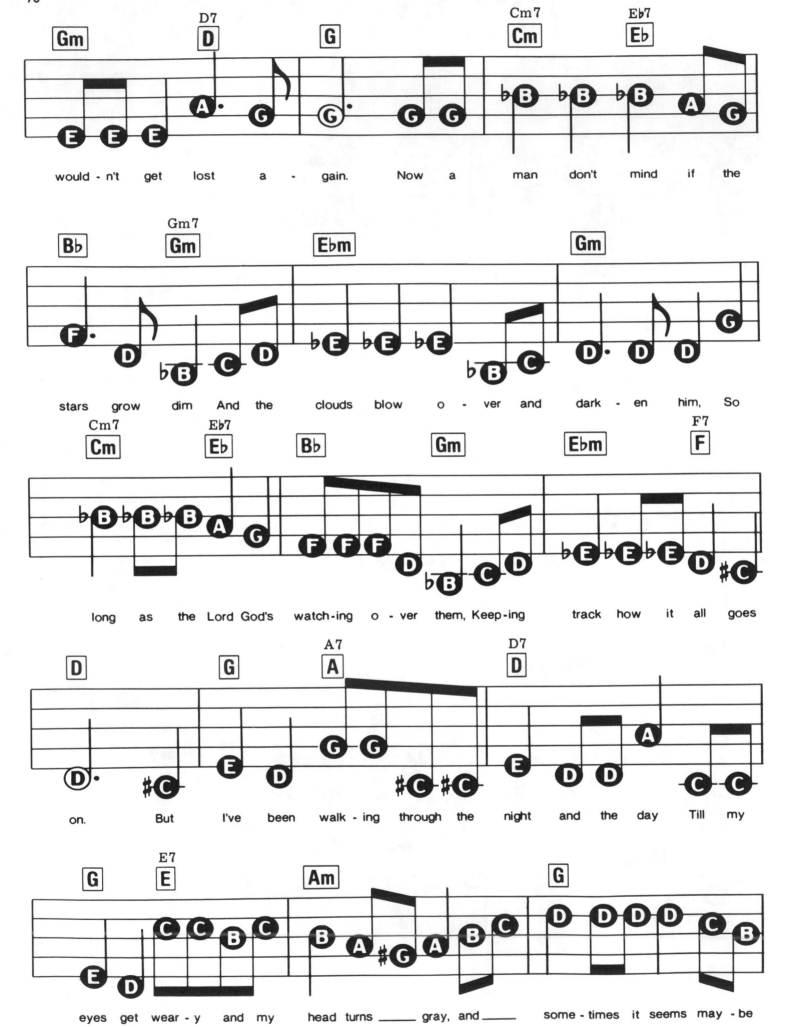

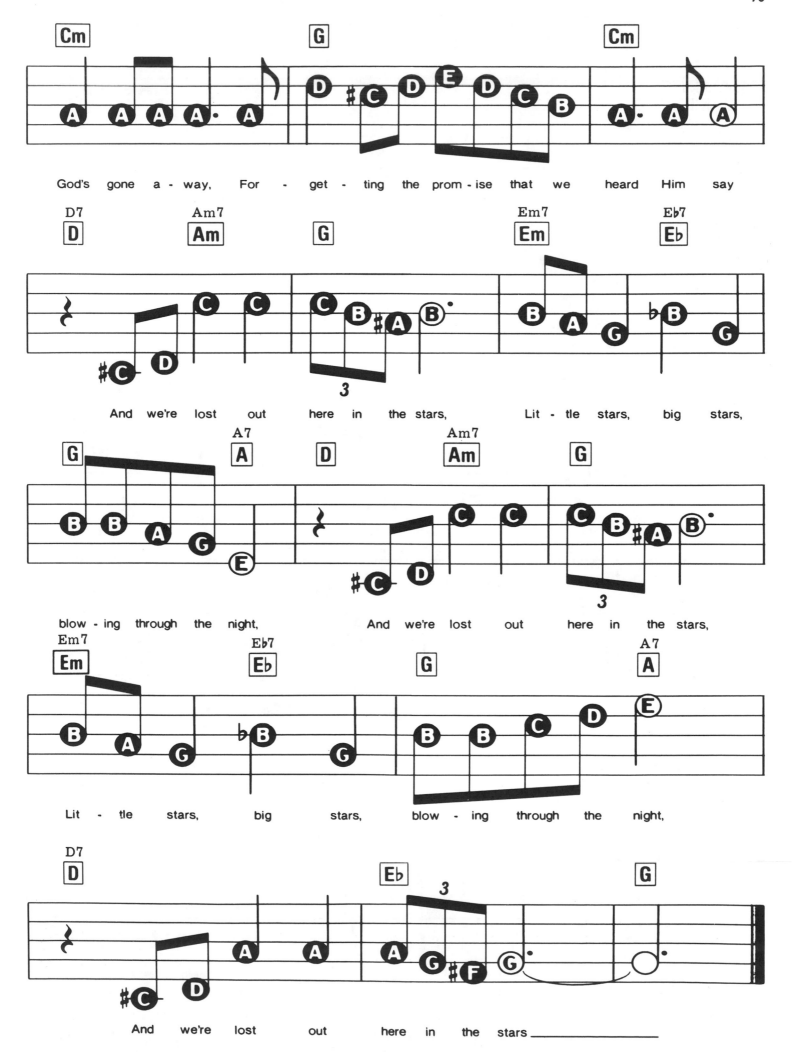

Maybe
from the Musical Production ANNIE

Registration 9
Rhythm: Fox Trot or Swing

Lyric by Martin Charnin
Music by Charles Strouse

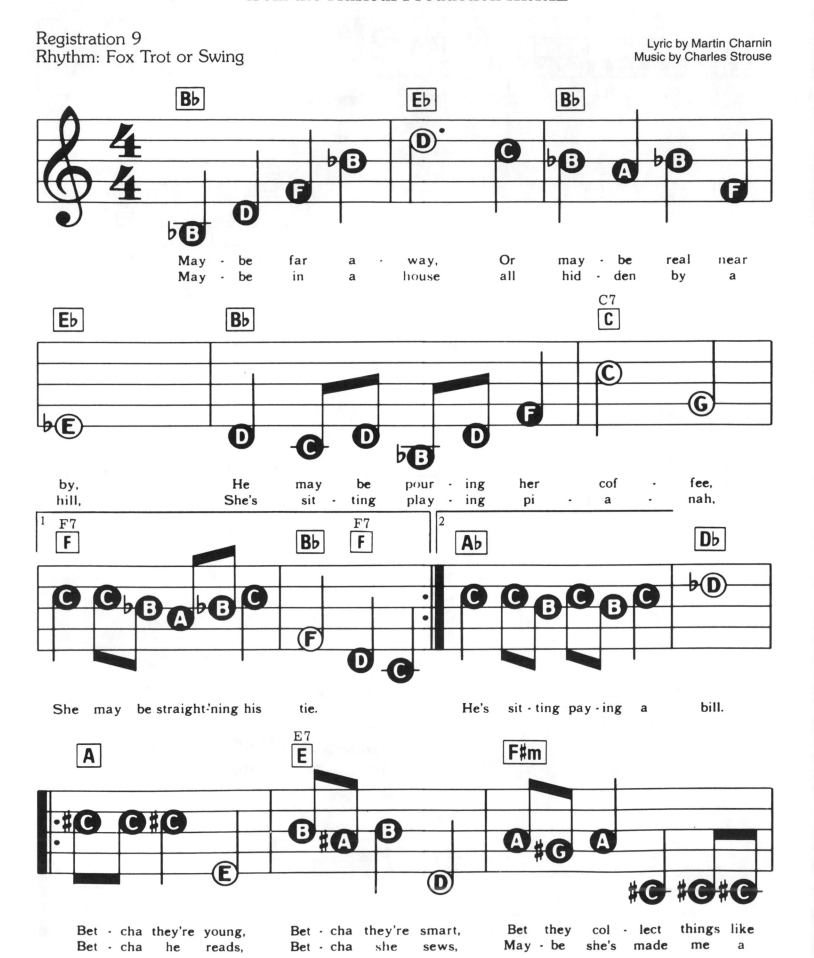

The Music of the Night
from THE PHANTOM OF THE OPERA

Registration 10
Rhythm: 8 Beat or Rock

Music by Andrew Lloyd Webber
Lyrics by Charles Hart
Additional Lyrics by Richard Stilgoe

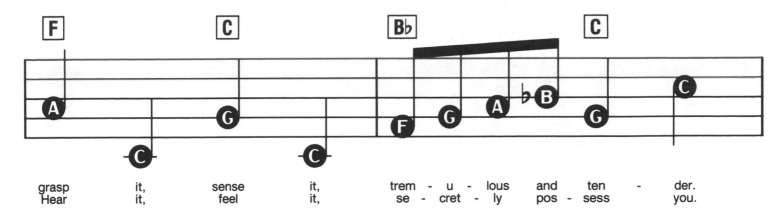

grasp   it,   sense   it,   trem - u - lous and ten - der.
Hear   it,   feel   it,   se - cret - ly pos - sess you.

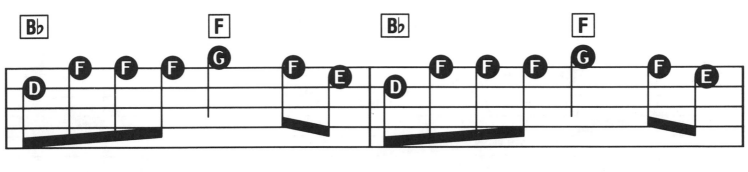

Turn your face a - way from the gar - ish light of day, turn your
O - pen up your mind, let your fan - ta - sies un - wind turn in the

thoughts a - way from cold un - feel - ing light   and
dark - ness which you know you can - not fight,   the

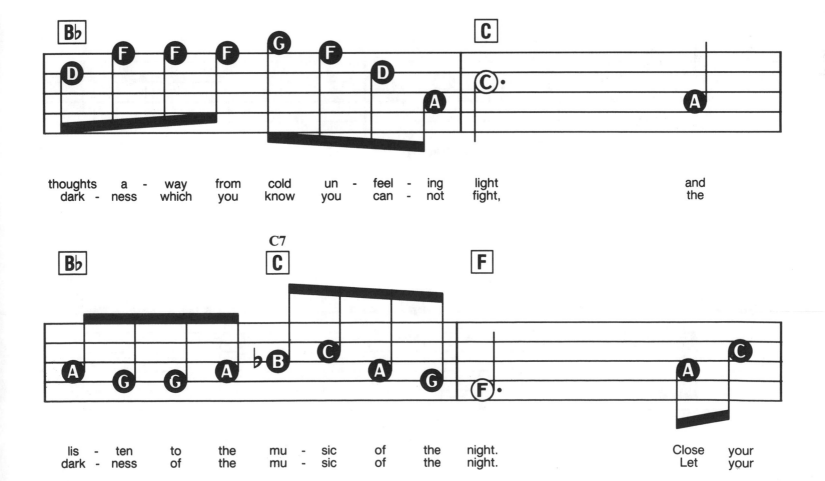

lis - ten to the mu - sic of the night.   Close your
dark - ness of the mu - sic of the night.   Let your

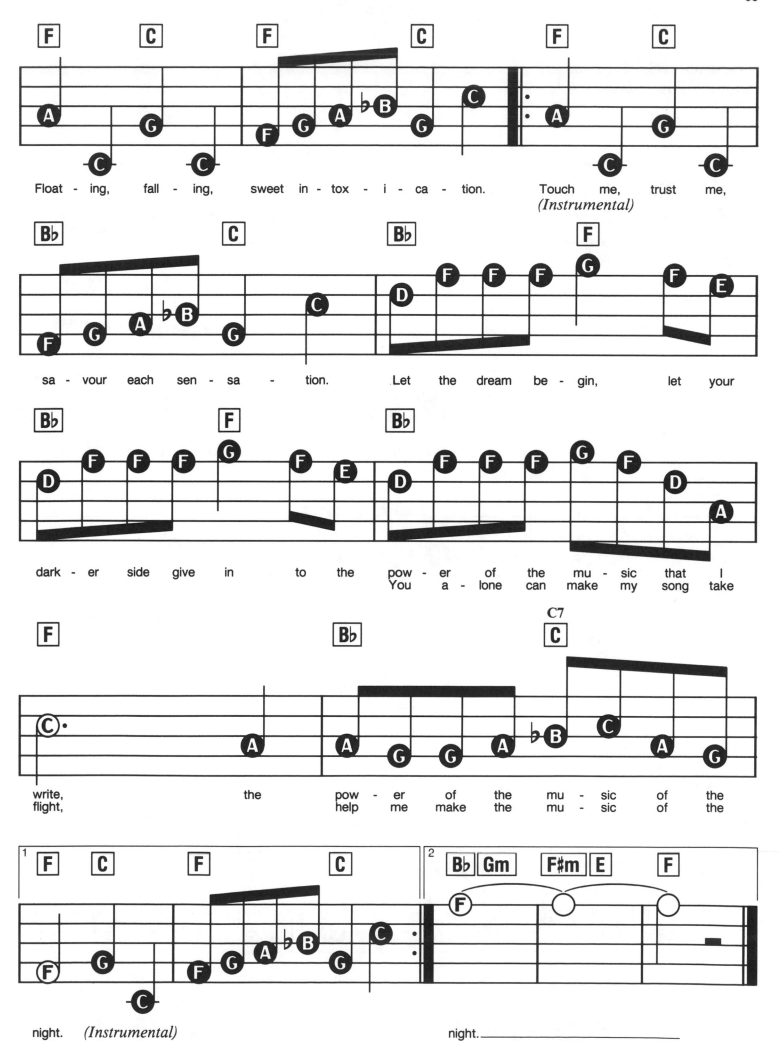

Float - ing, fall - ing, sweet in - tox - i - ca - tion. Touch me, trust me,
(Instrumental)

sa - vour each sen - sa - tion. Let the dream be - gin, let your

dark - er side give in to the pow - er of the mu - sic that I
You a - lone can make my song take

write, the pow - er of the mu - sic of the
flight, help me make the mu - sic of the

night. *(Instrumental)*

night._____

A New Life
from JEKYLL & HYDE

Registration 8
Rhythm: Broadway or 4/4 Ballad

Words by Leslie Bricusse
Music by Frank Wildhorn

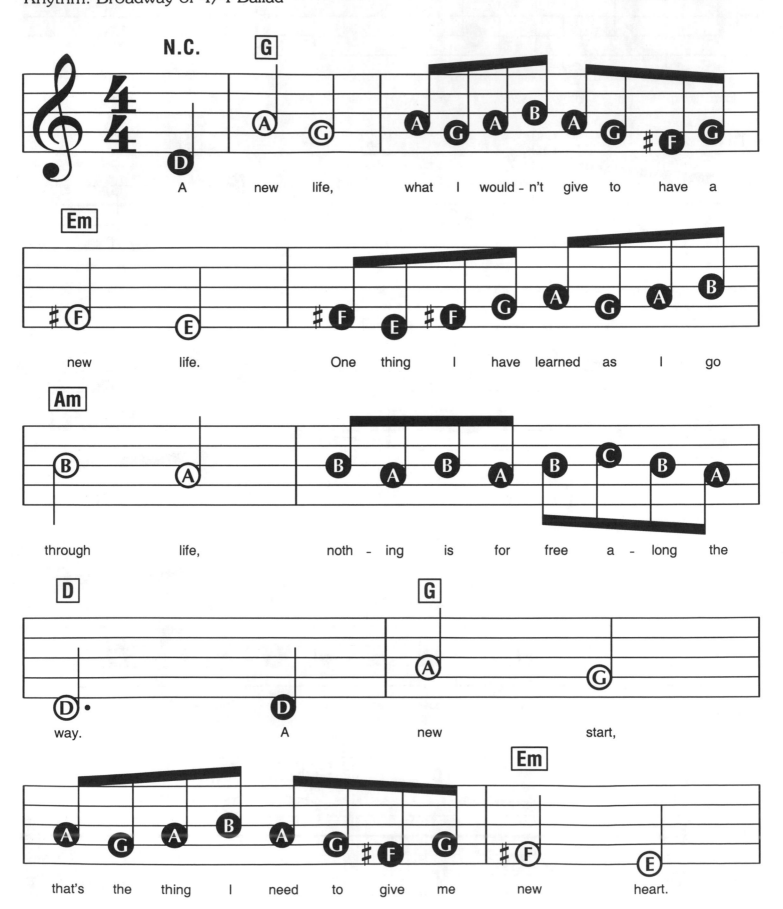

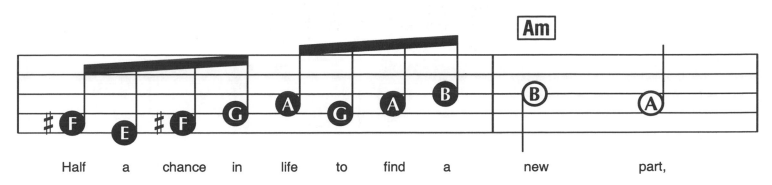

Half a chance in life to find a new part,

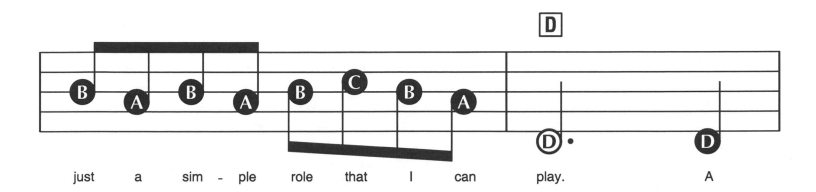

just a sim - ple role that I can play. A

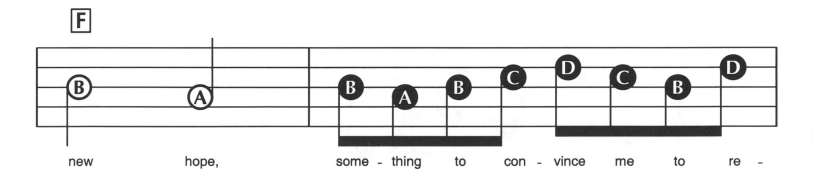

new hope, some - thing to con - vince me to re -

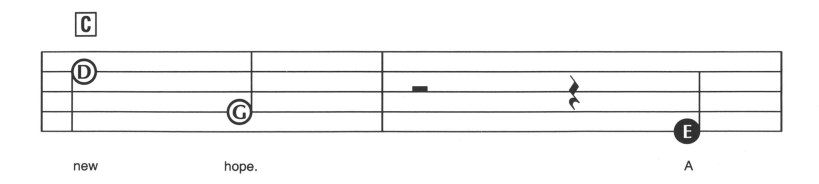

new hope. A

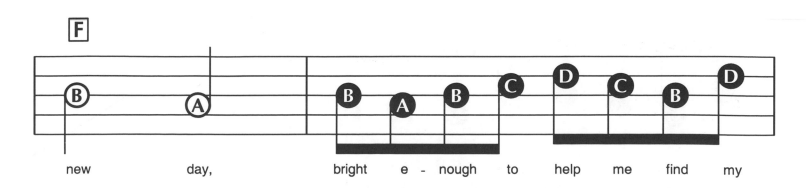

new day, bright e - nough to help me find my

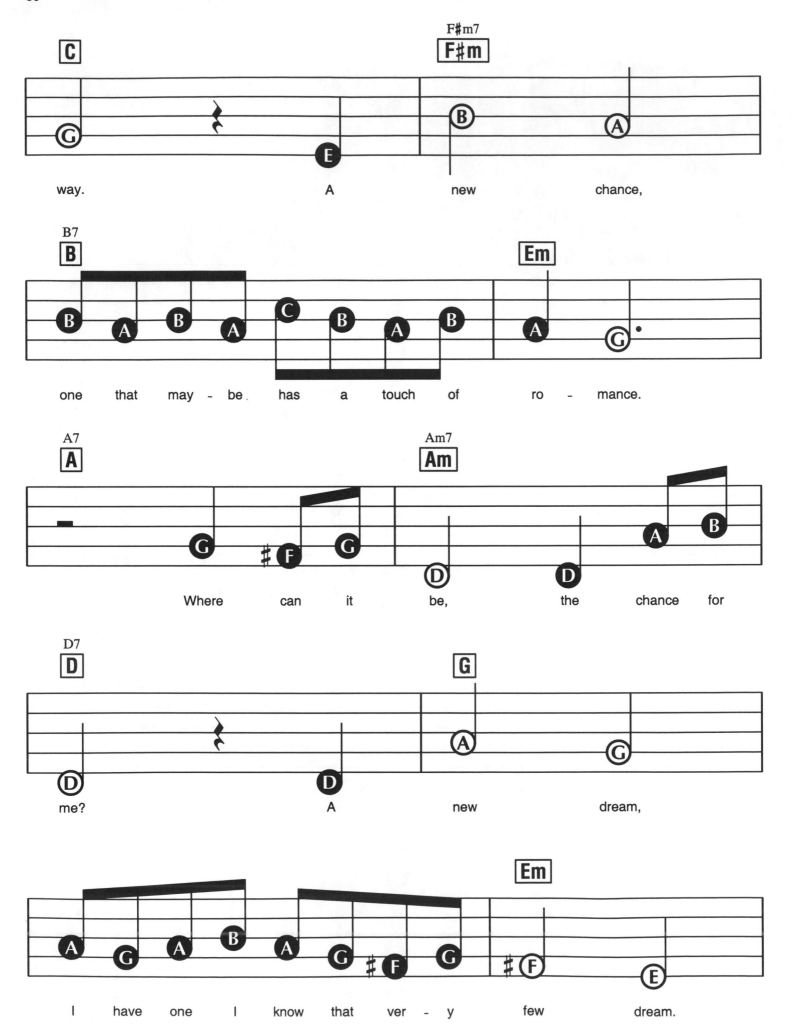

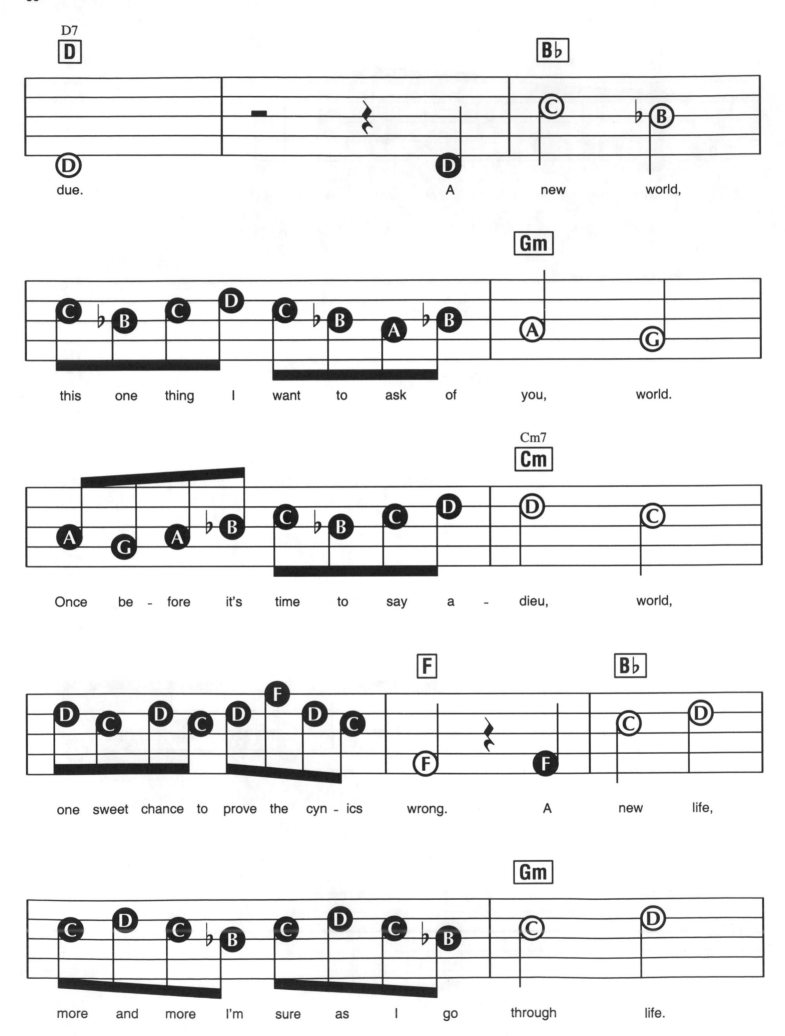

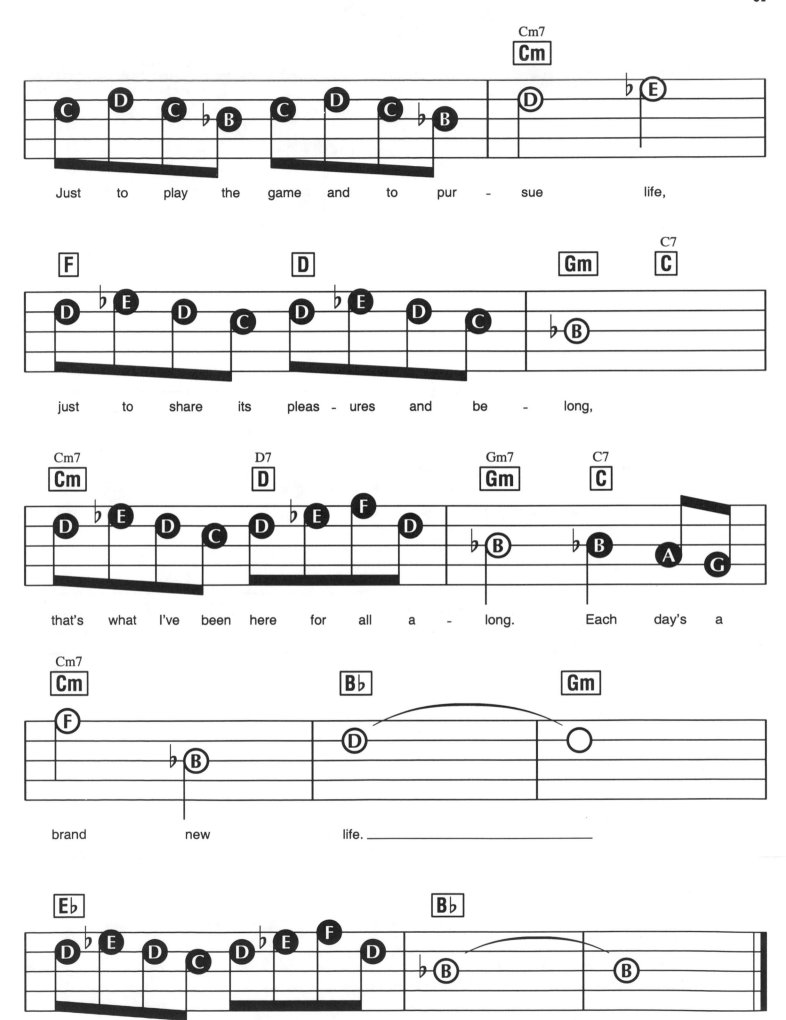

On My Own
from LES MISÉRABLES

Registration 1
Rhythm: Fox Trot or Ballad

Music by Claude-Michel Schönberg
Lyrics by Alain Boublil, Herbert Kretzmer, John Caird,
Trevor Nunn and Jean-Marc Natel

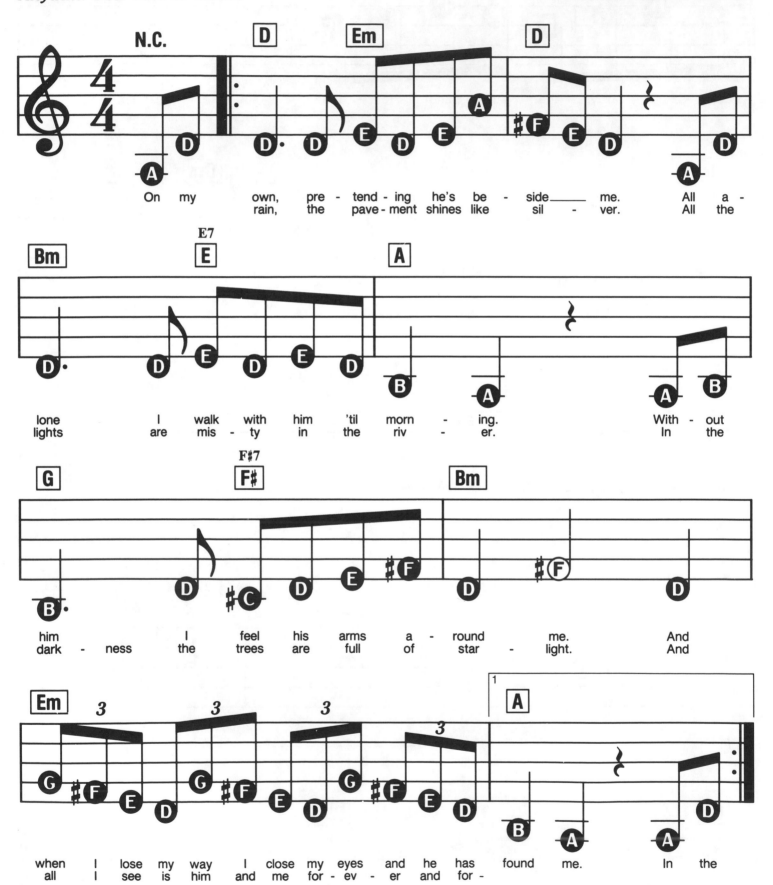

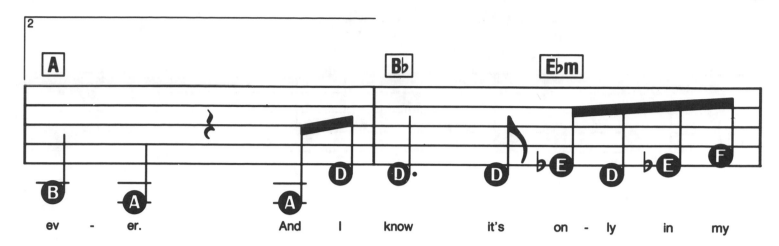

ev - er.   And I know it's on - ly in my

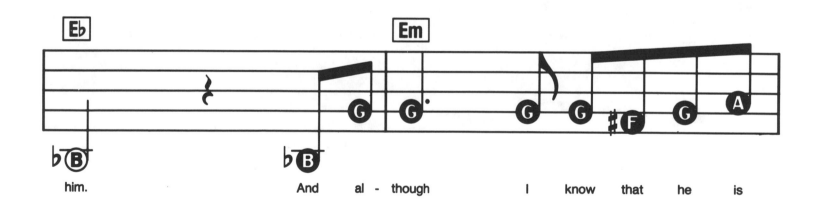

mind,   That I'm talk - ing to my - self and not to

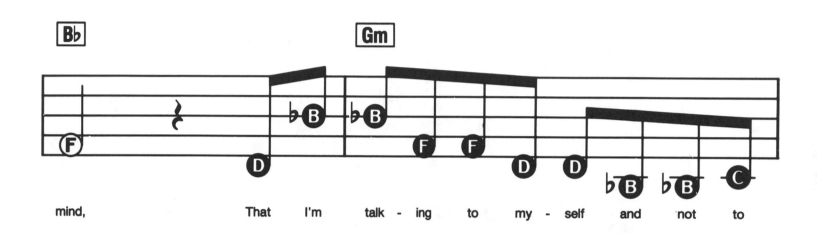

him.   And al - though I know that he is

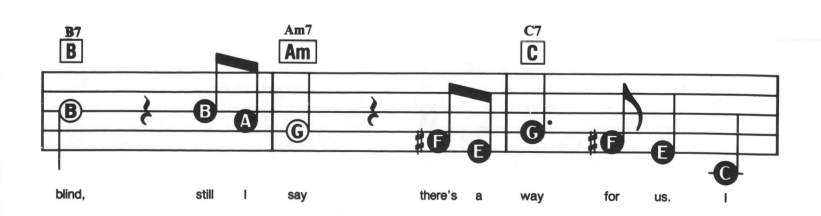

blind,   still I say   there's a way for us.   I

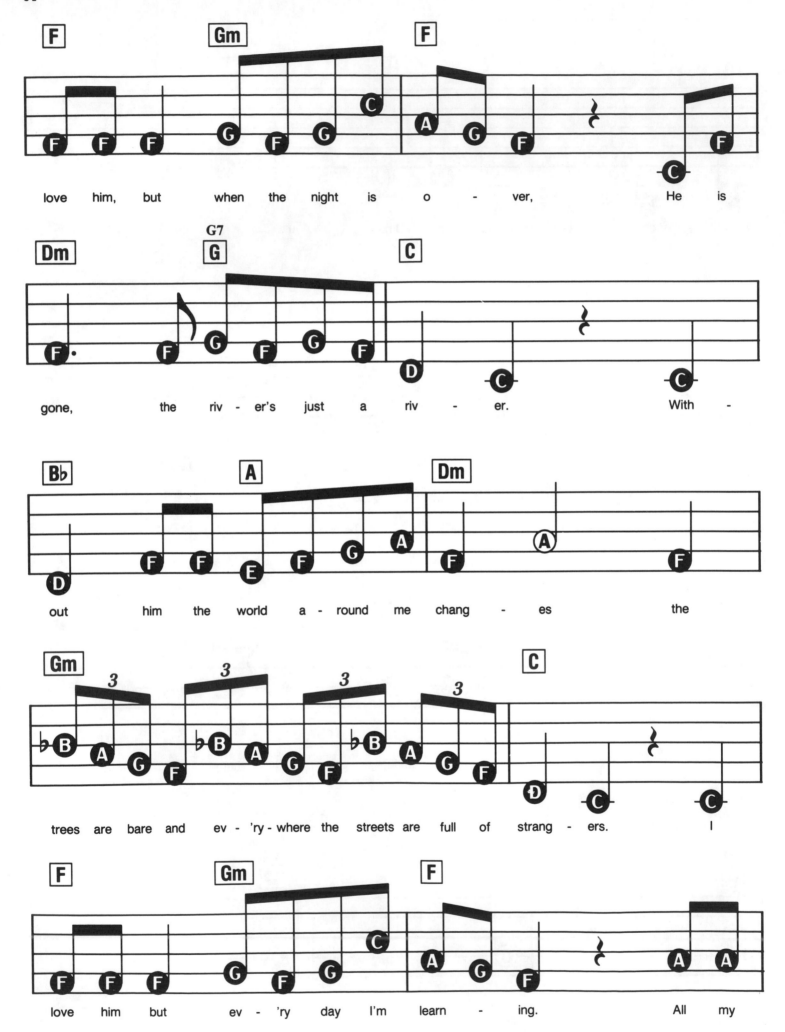

One
from A CHORUS LINE

Registration 5
Rhythm: Fox Trot or Swing

Music by Marvin Hamlisch
Lyric by Edward Kleban

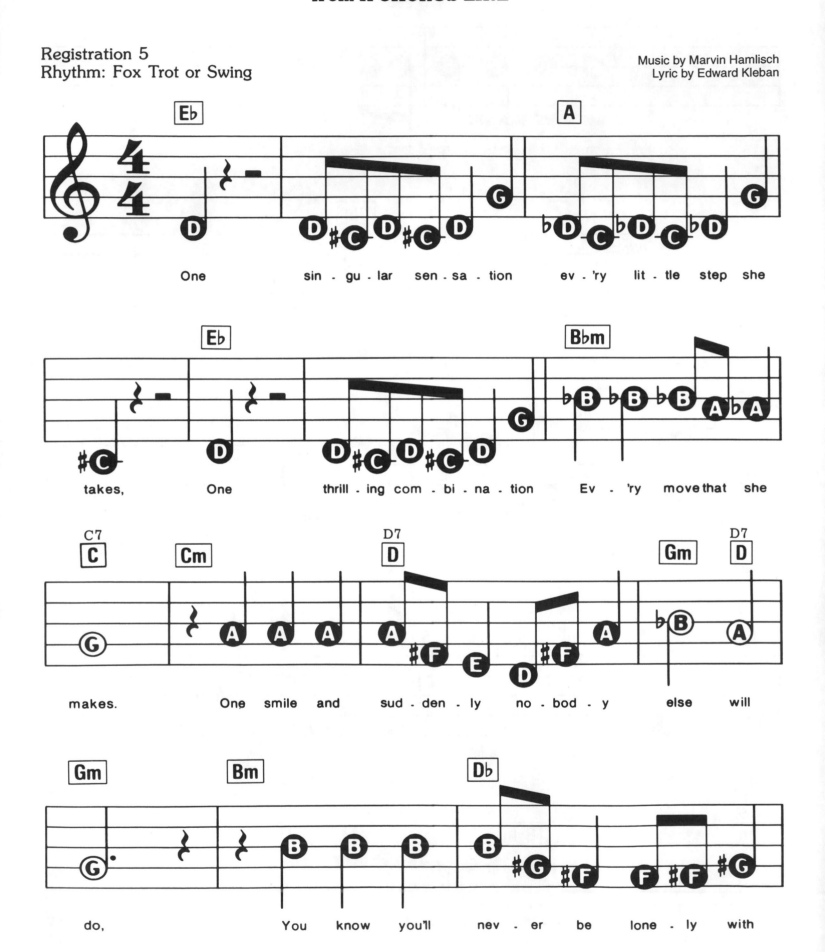

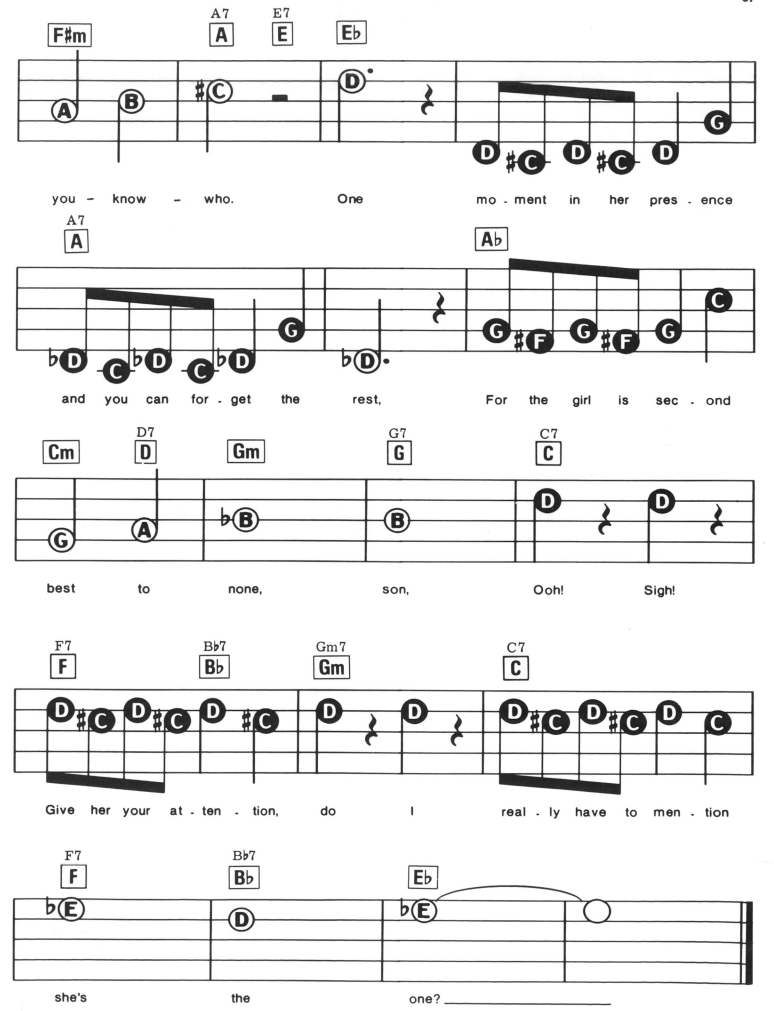

Out of My Dreams
from OKLAHOMA!

Registration 9
Rhythm: Waltz

Lyrics by Oscar Hammerstein II
Music by Richard Rodgers

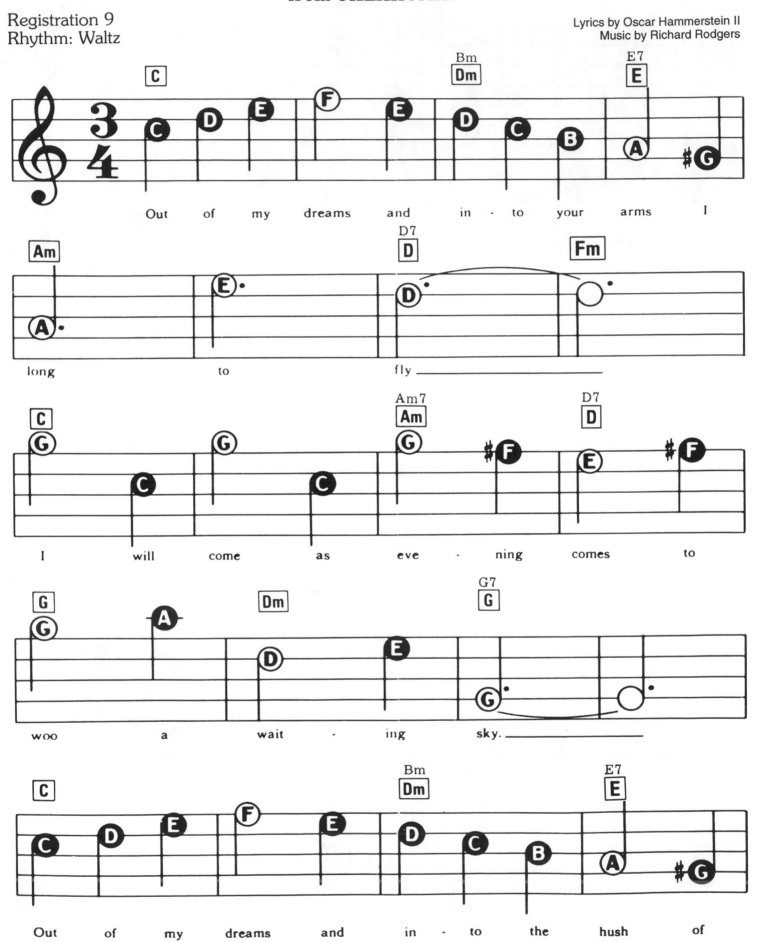

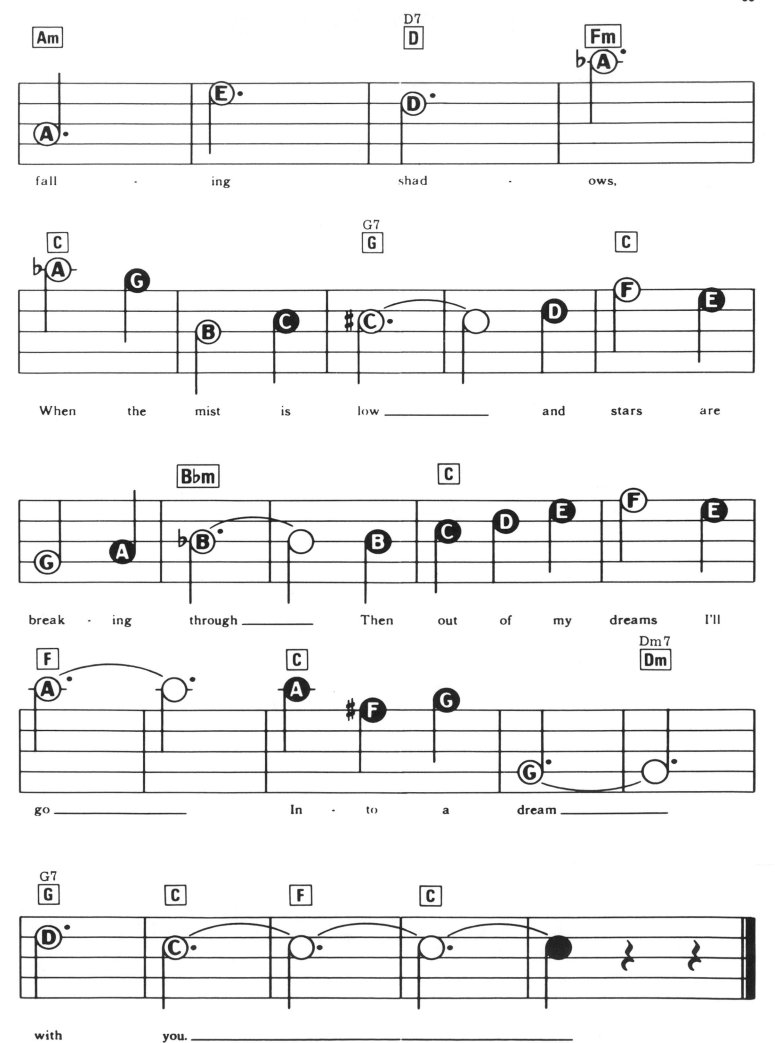

Seasons of Love
from RENT

Registration 5
Rhythm: Show Tunes or Fox Trot

Words and Music by
Jonathan Larson

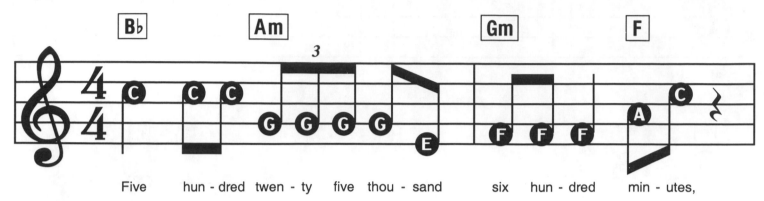

Five hun-dred twen-ty five thou-sand six hun-dred min-utes,

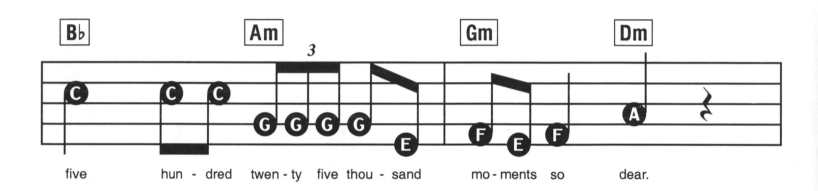

five hun-dred twen-ty five thou-sand mo-ments so dear.

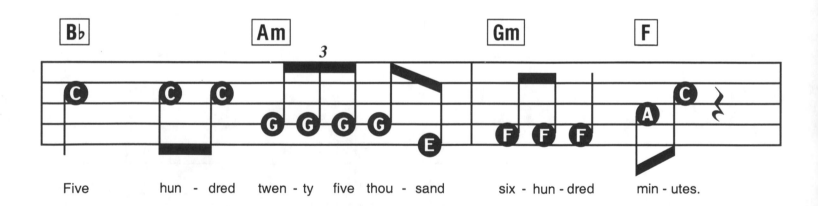

Five hun-dred twen-ty five thou-sand six-hun-dred min-utes.

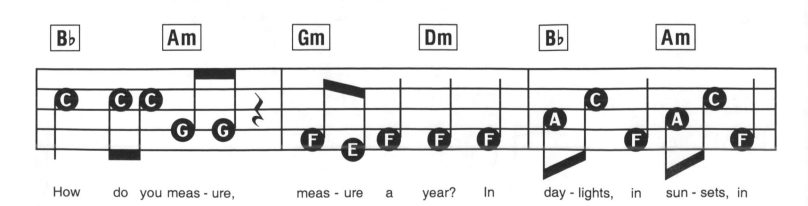

How do you meas-ure, meas-ure a year? In day-lights, in sun-sets, in

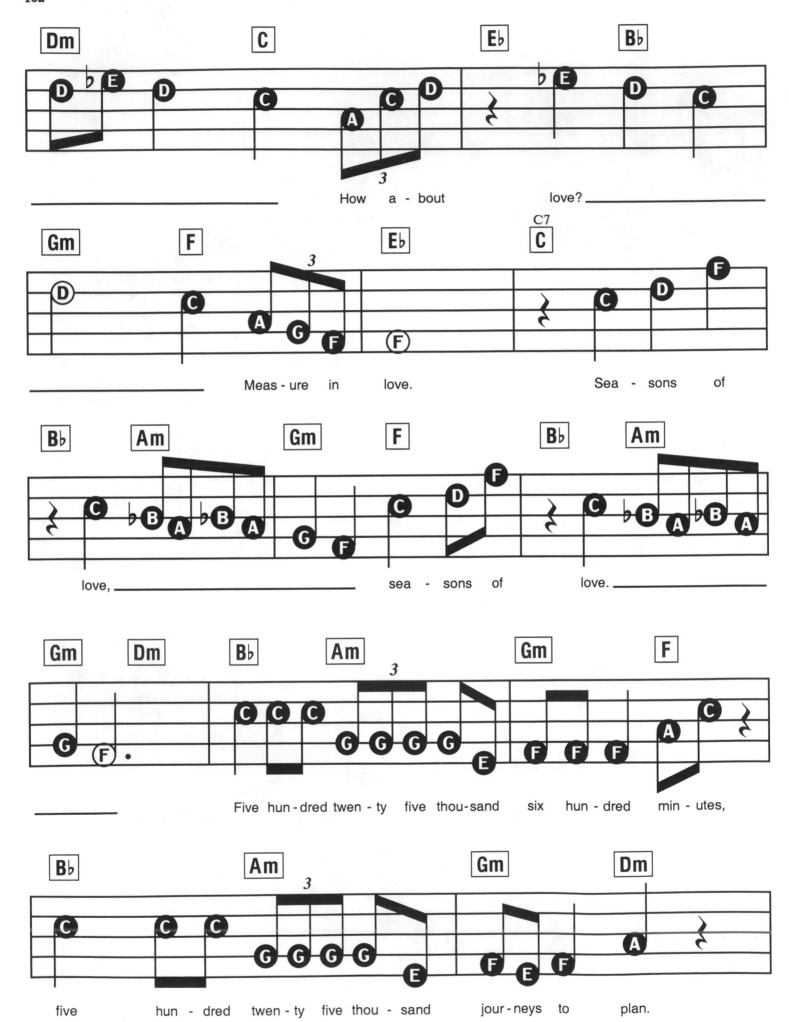

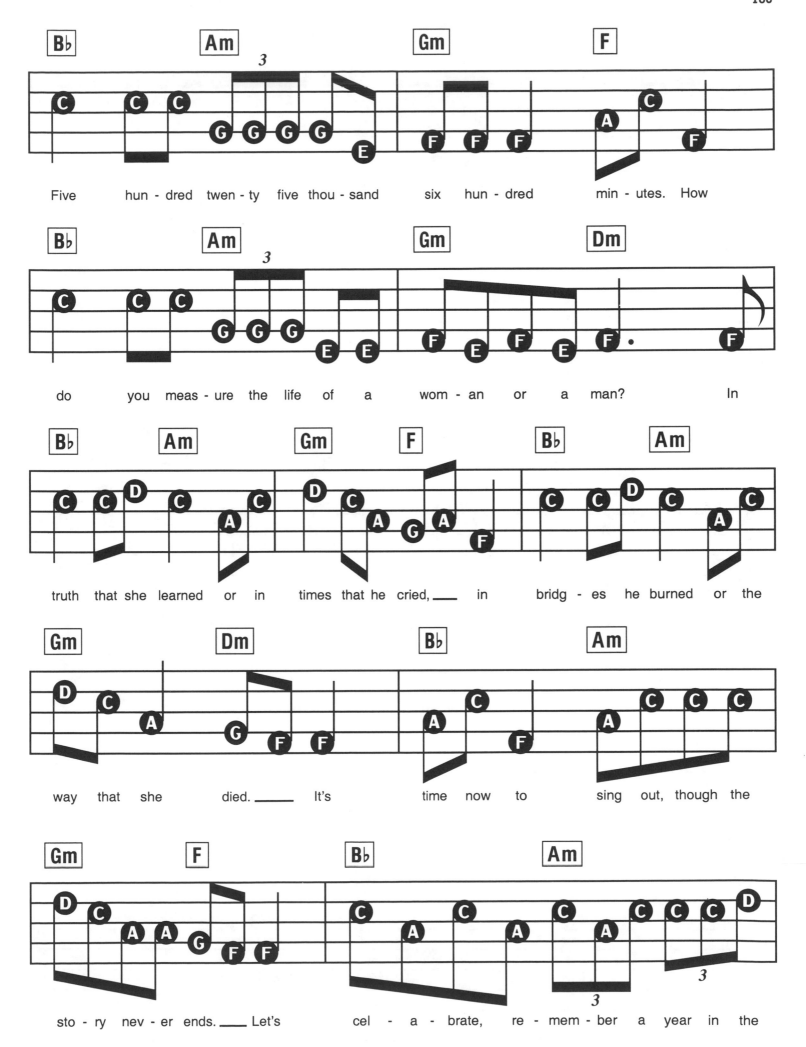

104

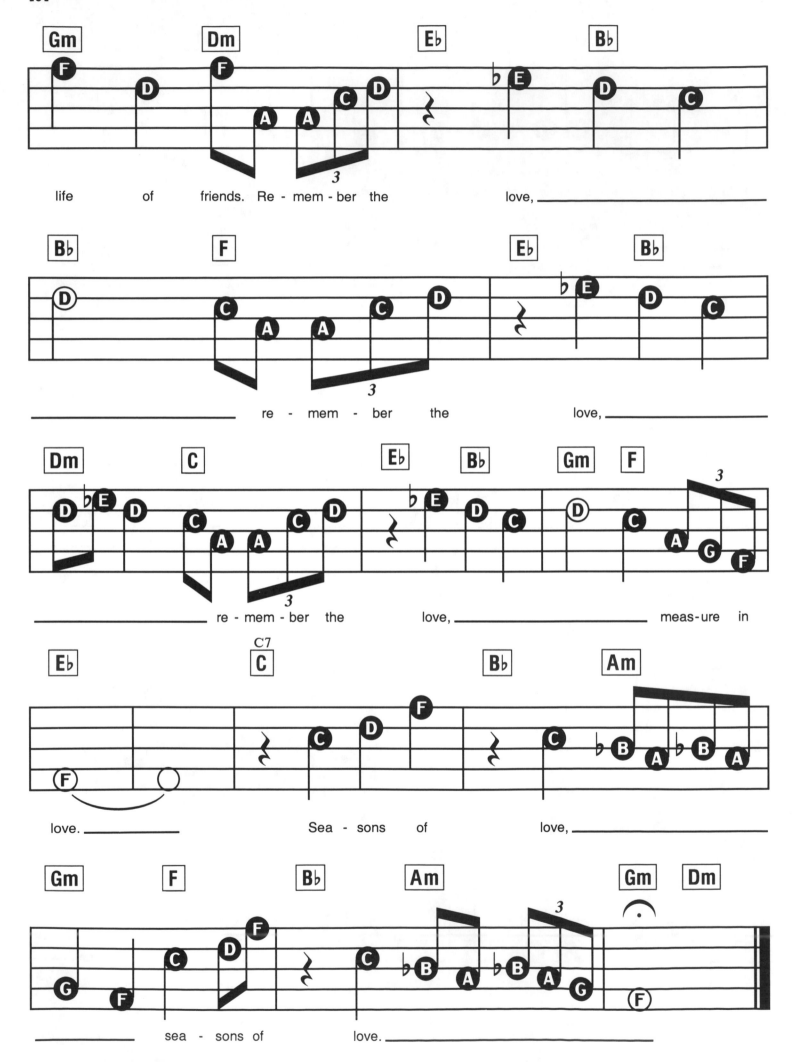

Some Enchanted Evening
from SOUTH PACIFIC

Registration 1
Rhythm: Broadway or Fox Trot

Lyrics by Oscar Hammerstein II
Music by Richard Rodgers

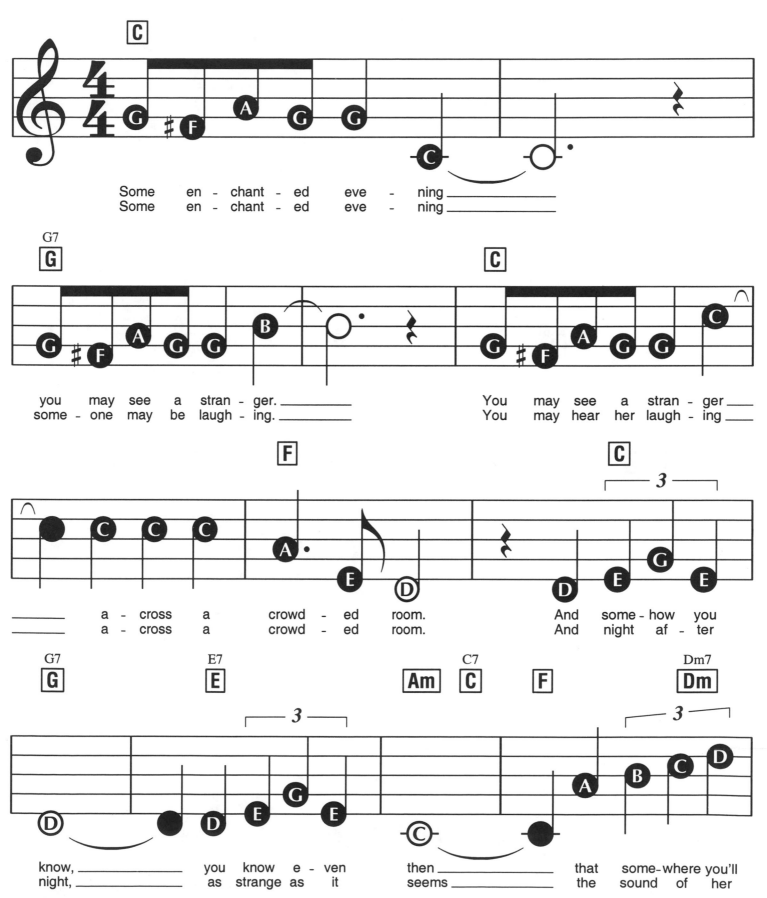

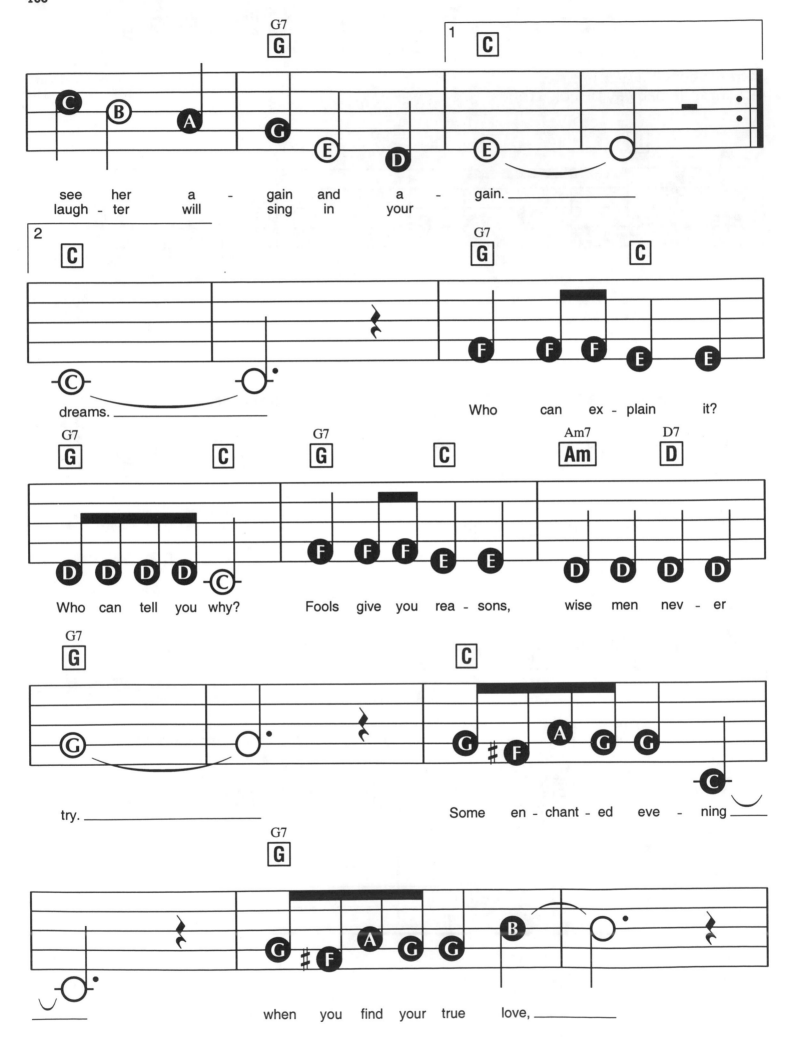

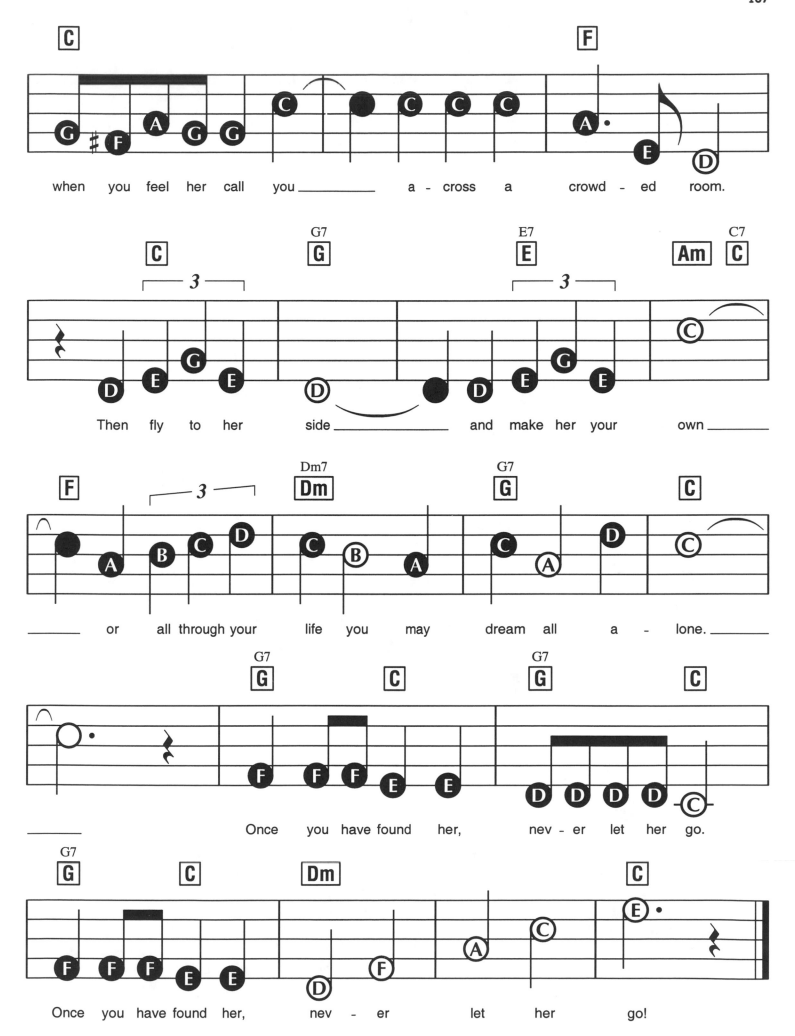

September Song
from the Musical Play KNICKERBOCKER HOLIDAY

Registration 2
Rhythm: Fox Trot

Words by Maxwell Anderson
Music by Kurt Weill

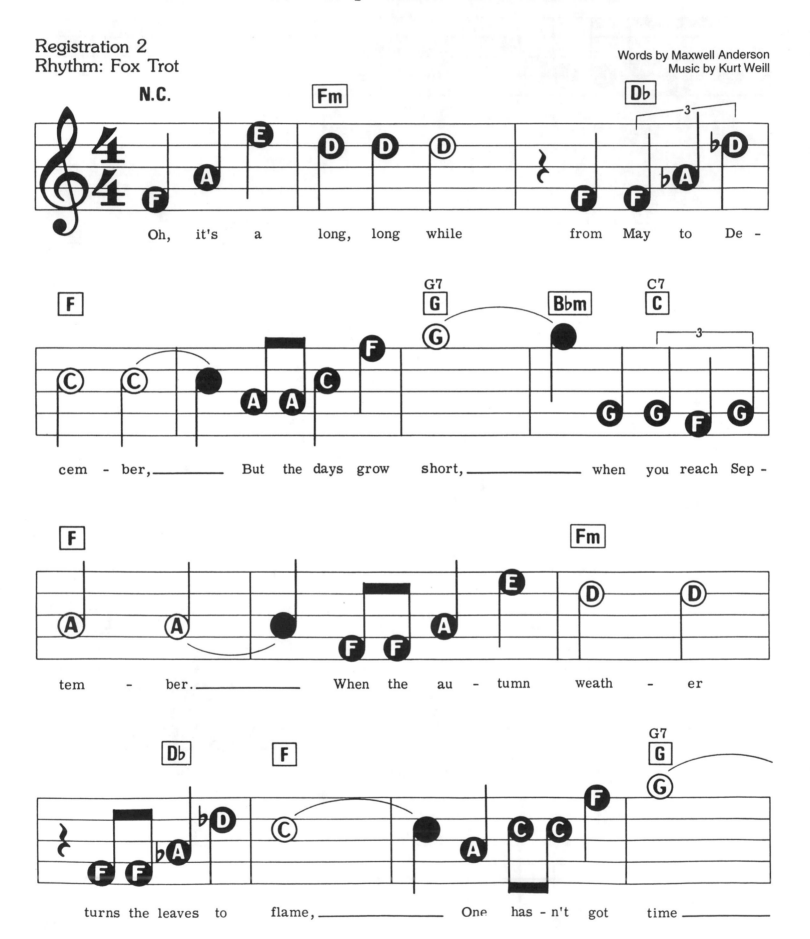

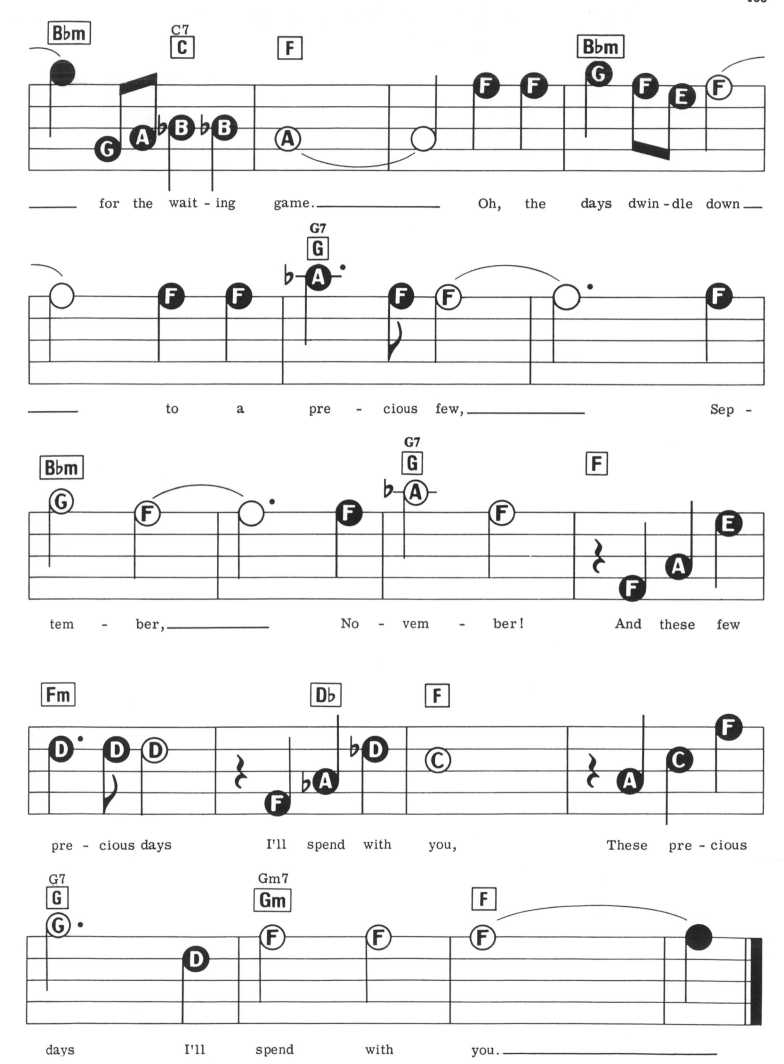

Seventy Six Trombones
from Meredith Willson's THE MUSIC MAN

Registration 5
Rhythm: 6/8 March

By Meredith Willson

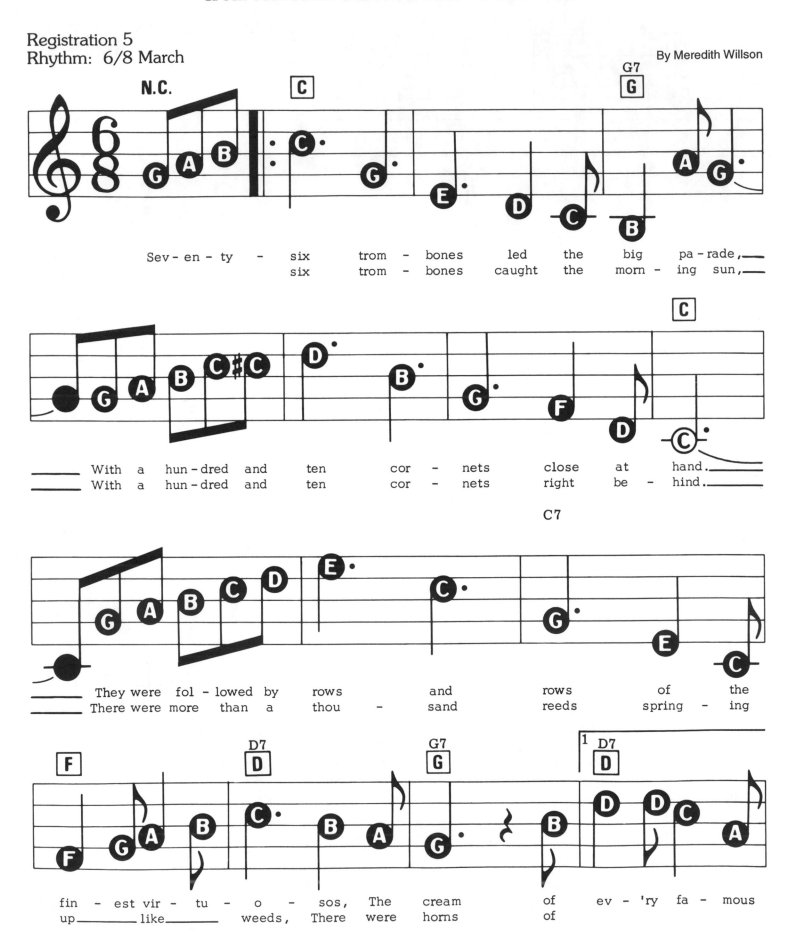

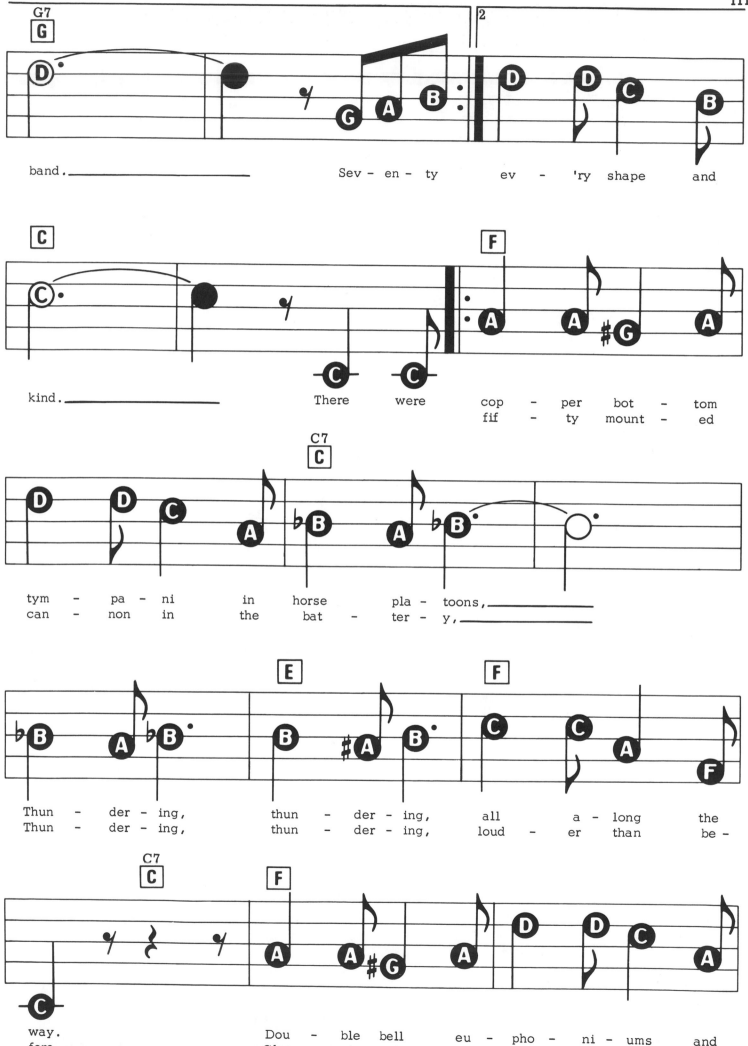

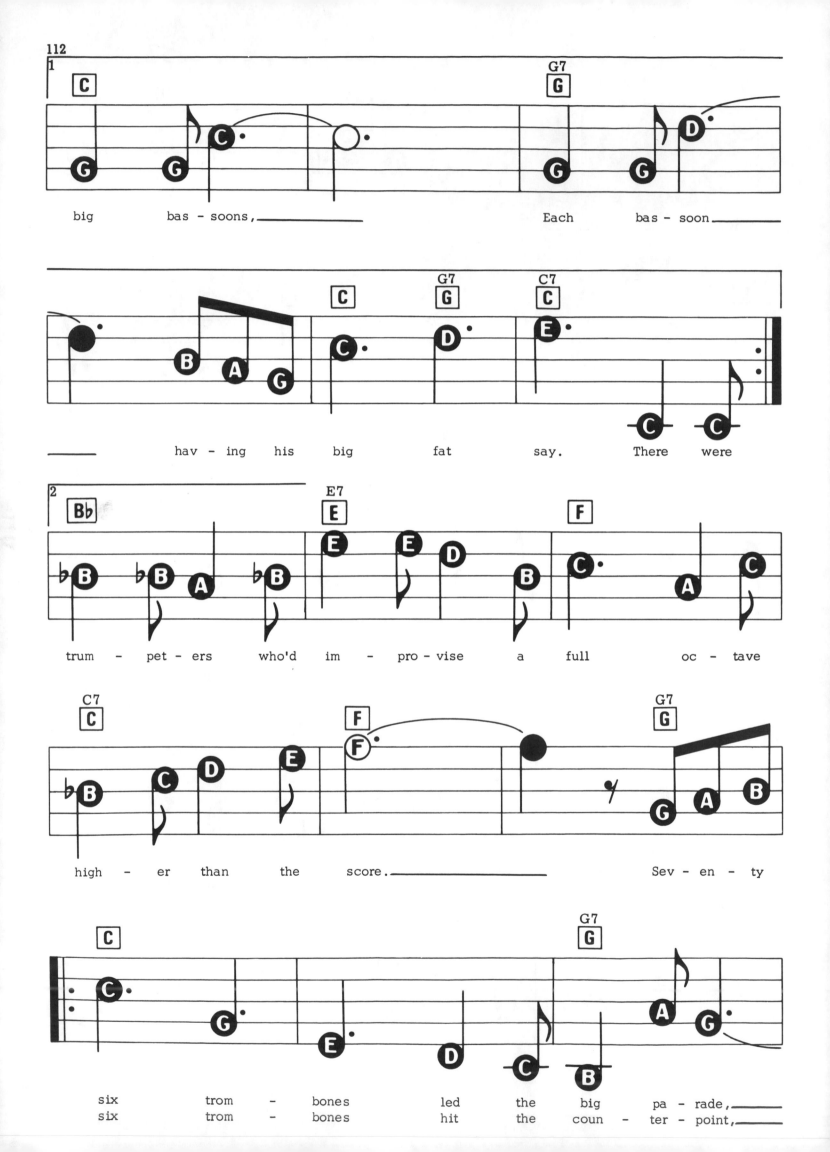

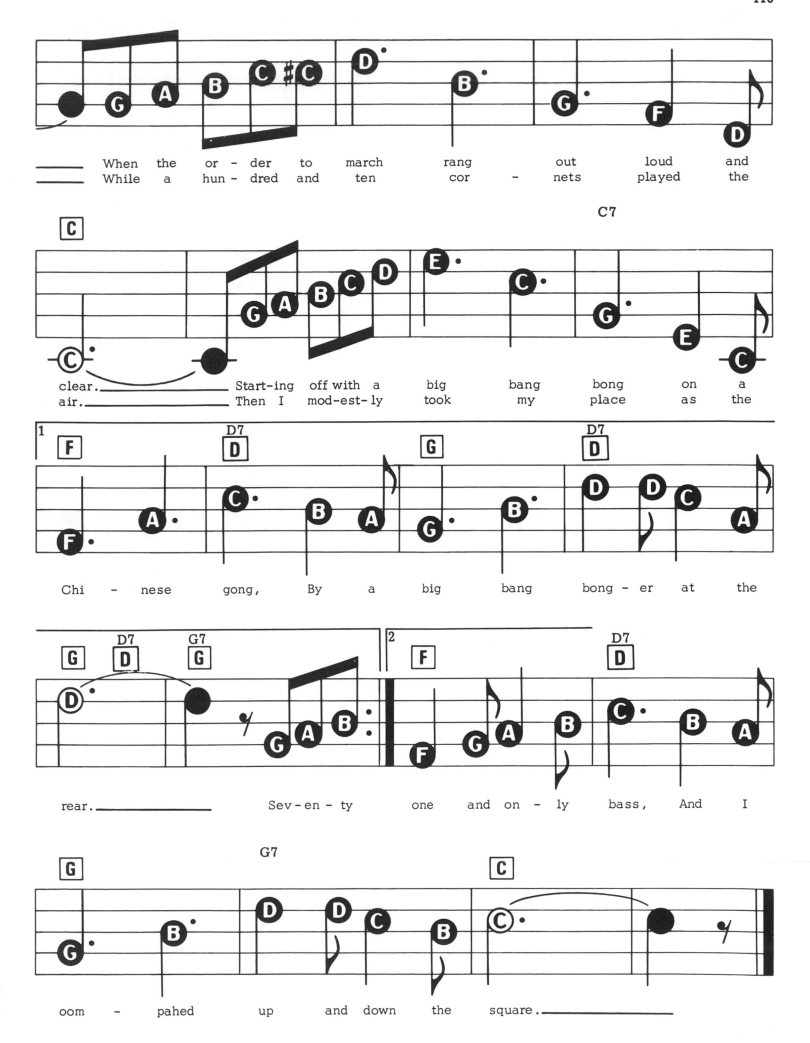

Sit Down You're Rockin' the Boat

from GUYS AND DOLLS

Registration 7
Rhythm: Broadway or Fox Trot

By Frank Loesser

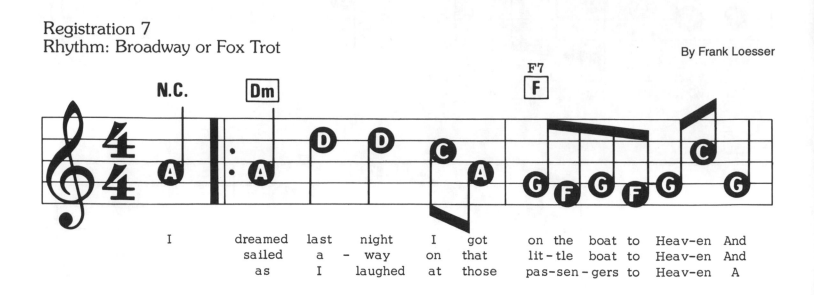

I dreamed last night I got on the boat to Heav-en And
sailed last a-way on that lit-tle boat to Heav-en And
as I laughed at those pas-sen-gers to Heav-en A

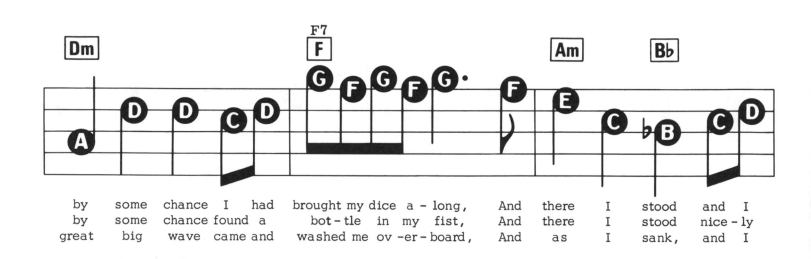

by some chance I had brought my dice a-long, And there I stood and I
by some chance found a bot-tle in my fist, And there I stood nice-ly
great big wave came and washed me ov-er-board, And as I sank, and I

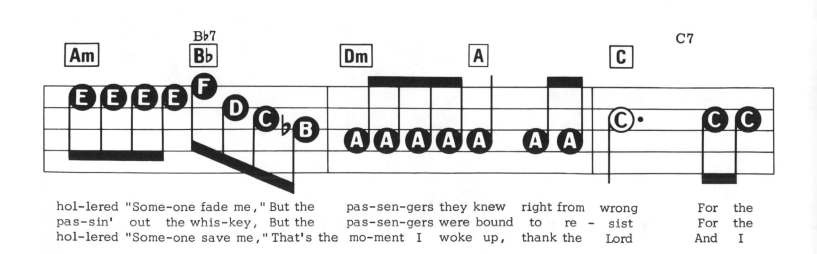

hol-lered "Some-one fade me," But the pas-sen-gers they knew right from wrong For the
pas-sin' out the whis-key, But the pas-sen-gers were bound to re-sist For the
hol-lered "Some-one save me," That's the mo-ment I woke up, thank the Lord And I

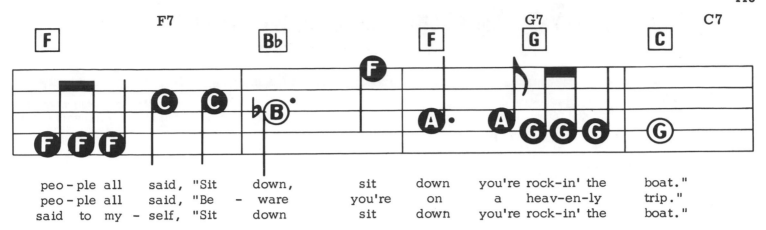

peo - ple all said, "Sit down, sit down you're rock-in' the boat."
peo - ple all said, "Be - ware you're on a heav-en-ly trip."
said to my - self, "Sit down sit down you're rock-in' the boat."

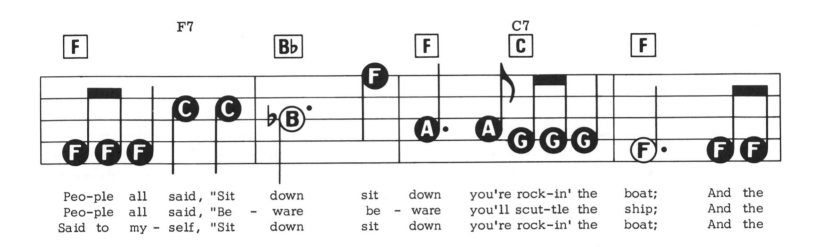

Peo - ple all said, "Sit down sit down you're rock-in' the boat; And the
Peo - ple all said, "Be - ware be - ware you'll scut-tle the ship; And the
Said to my - self, "Sit down sit down you're rock-in' the boat; And the

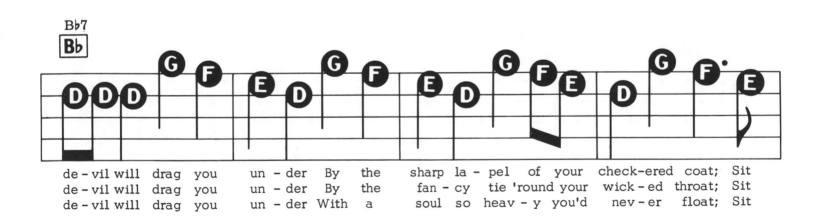

de - vil will drag you un - der By the sharp la - pel of your check-ered coat; Sit
de - vil will drag you un - der By the fan - cy tie 'round your wick-ed throat; Sit
de - vil will drag you un - der With a soul so heav - y you'd nev-er float; Sit

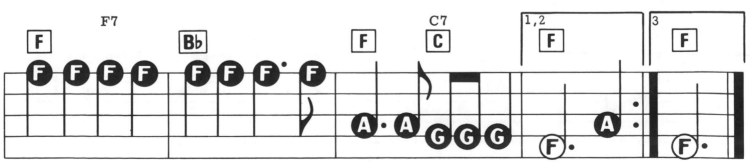

down, sit down, sit down sit down, Sit down you're rock-in' the boat." I
down, sit down, sit down sit down, Sit down you're rock-in' the boat." And
down, sit down, sit down sit down, Sit down you're rock-in' the boat."

So Long, Farewell

from THE SOUND OF MUSIC

Registration 3
Rhythm: Polka or Fox Trot

Lyrics by Oscar Hammerstein II
Music by Richard Rodgers

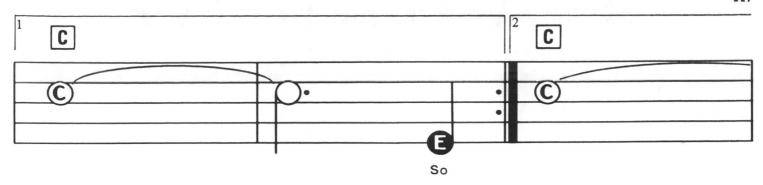

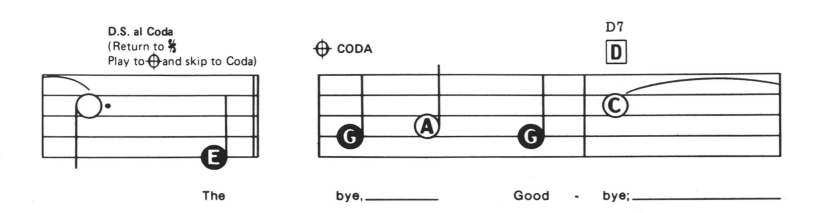

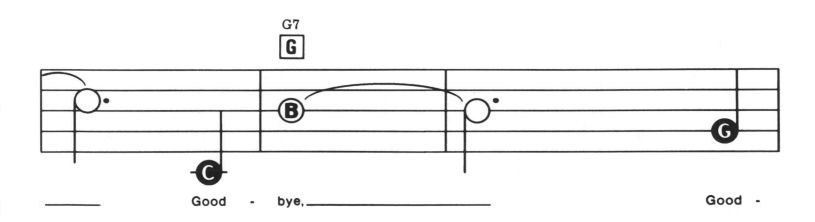

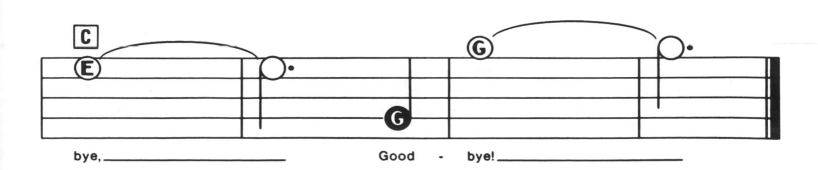

Somebody, Somewhere
from THE MOST HAPPY FELLA

Registration 8
Rhythm: Broadway or 4/4 Ballad

By Frank Loesser

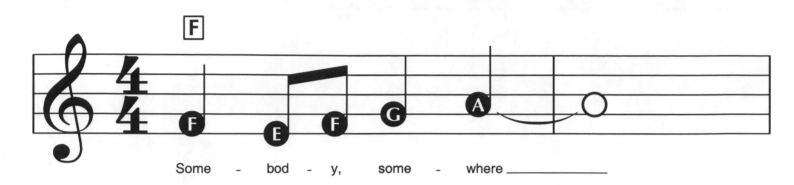

Some - bod - y, some - where _____

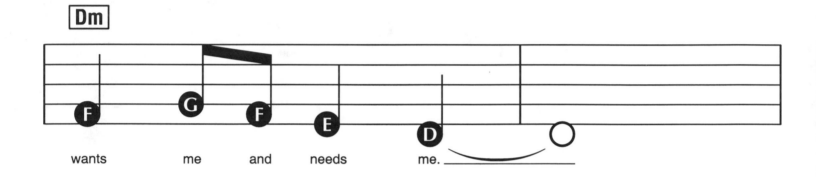

wants   me   and   needs   me. _____

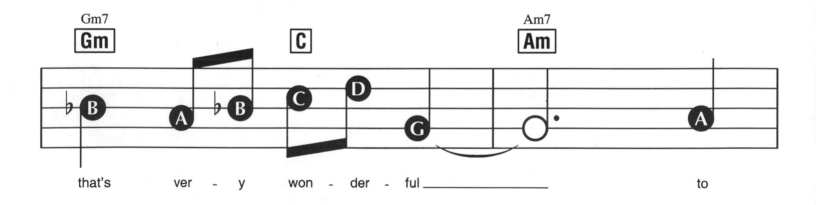

that's   ver - y   won - der - ful _____   to

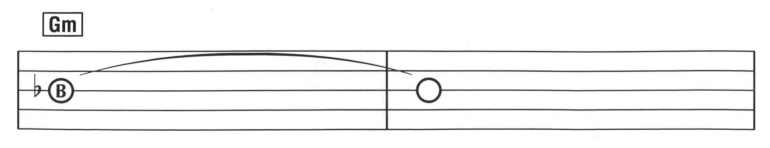

know. _____

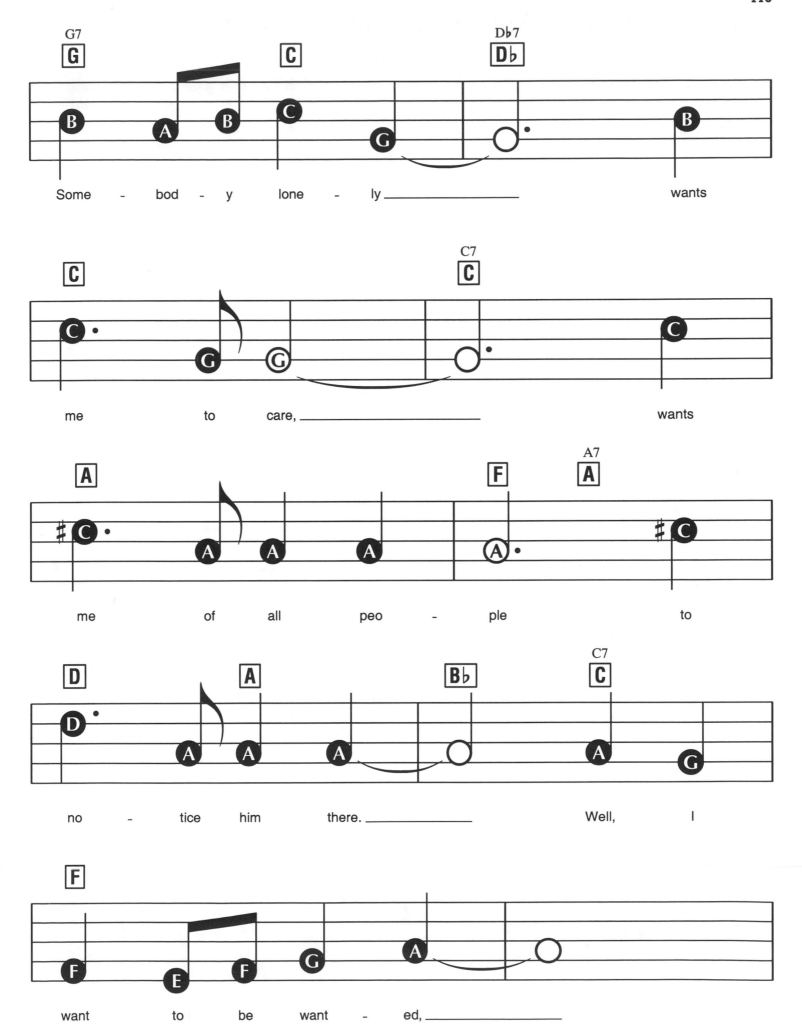

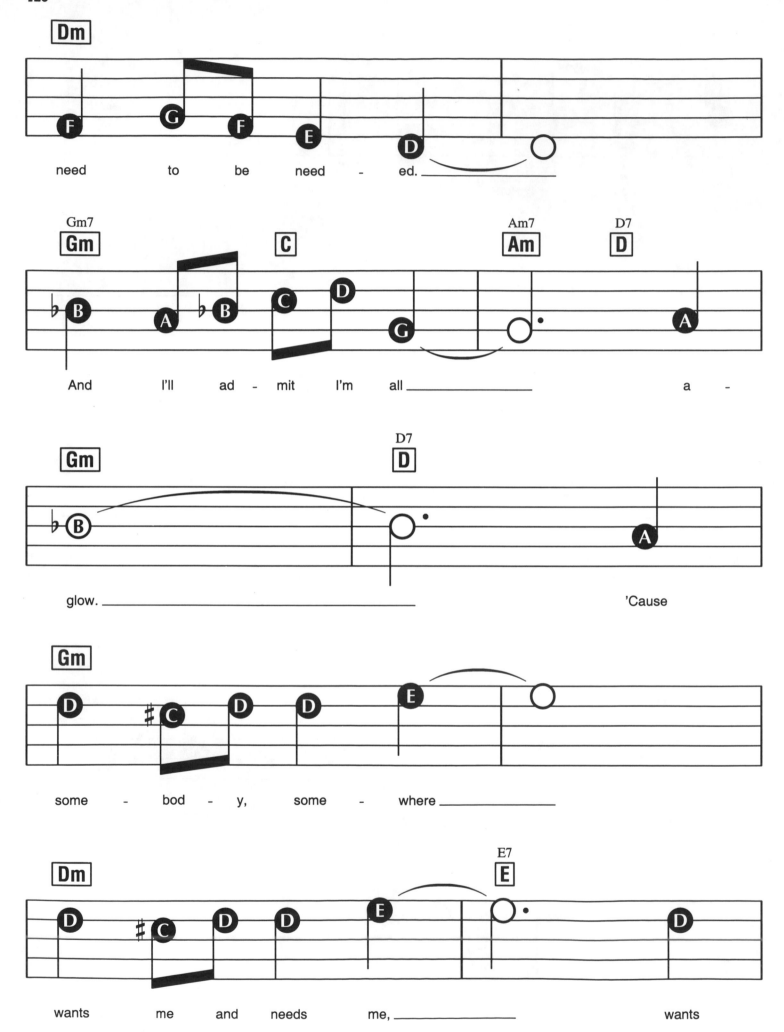

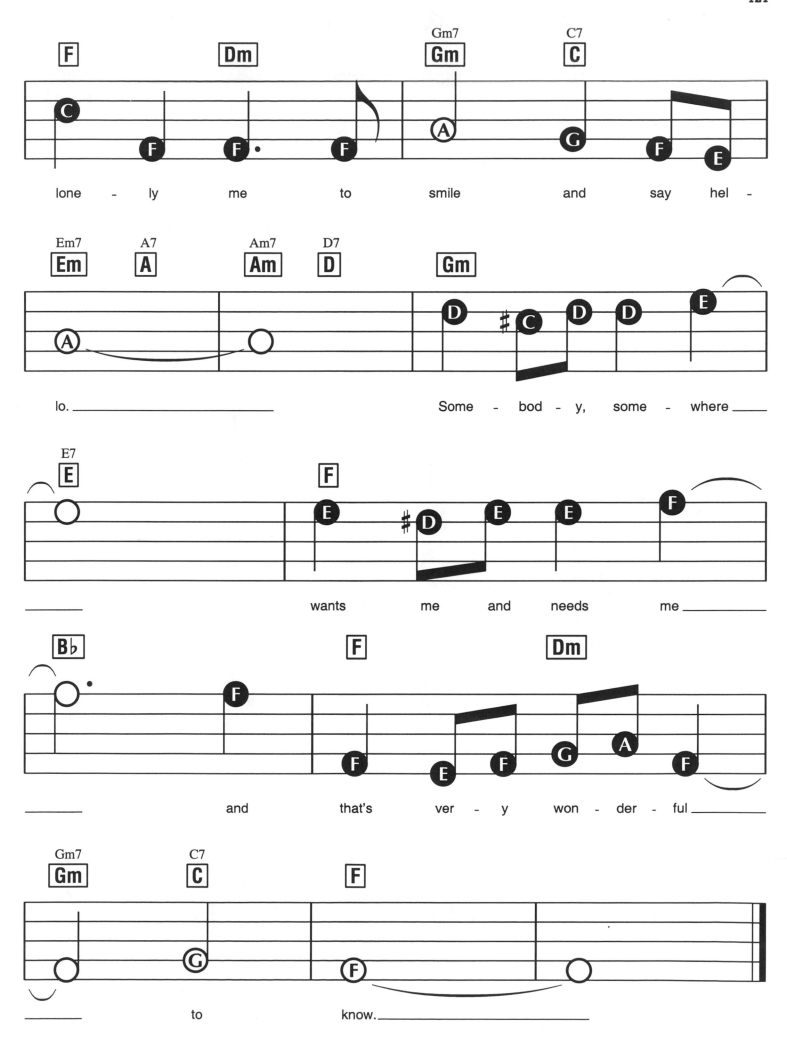

Something Wonderful
from THE KING AND I

Registration 10
Rhythm: Fox Trot or Swing

Lyrics by Oscar Hammerstein II
Music by Richard Rodgers

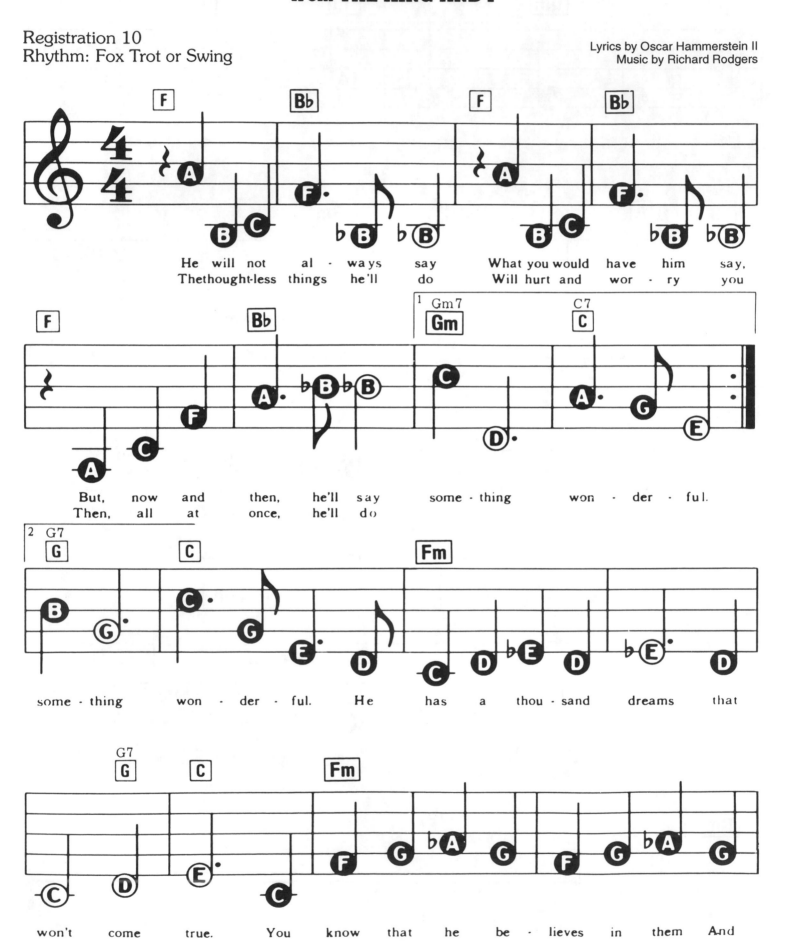

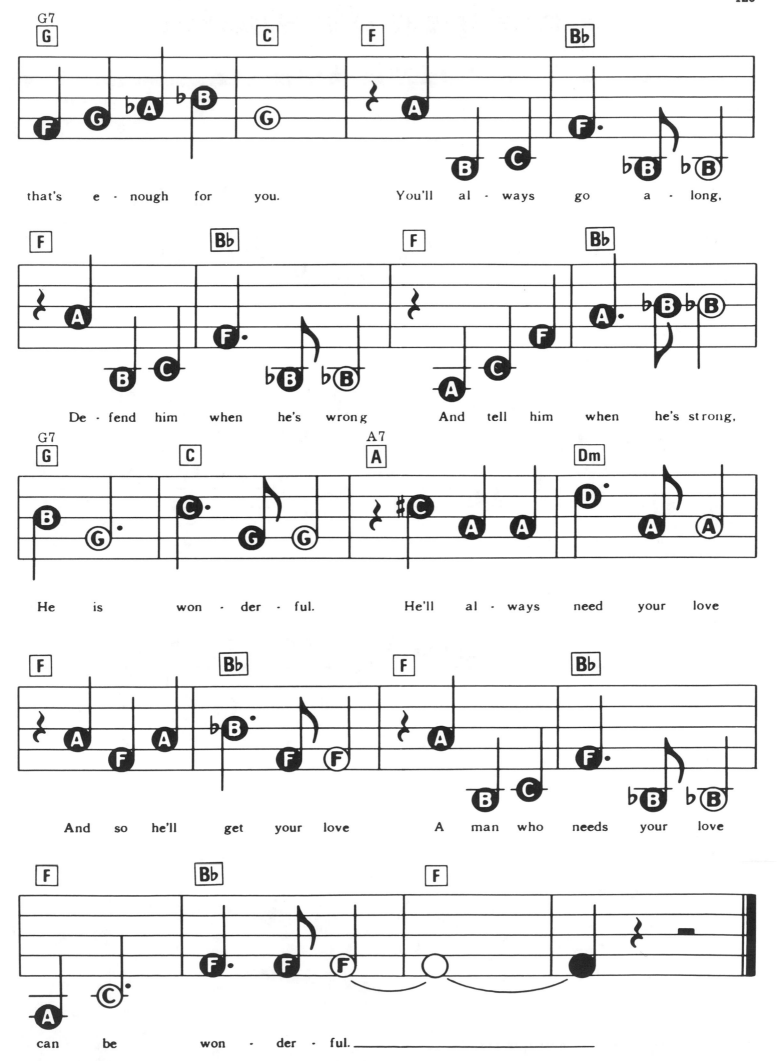

Song on the Sand
(La Da Da Da)
from LA CAGE AUX FOLLES

Registration 1
Rhythm: Pops or 8 Beat

Music and Lyric by
Jerry Herman

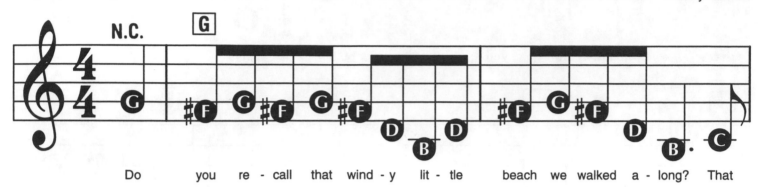

Do you re-call that wind-y lit-tle beach we walked a-long? That

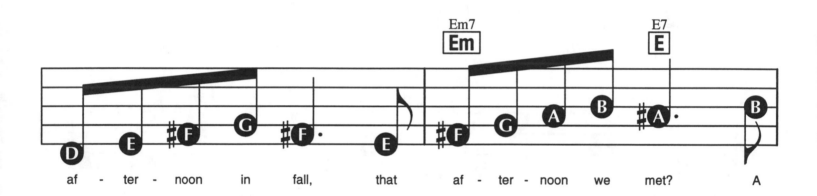

af-ter-noon in fall, that af-ter-noon we met? A

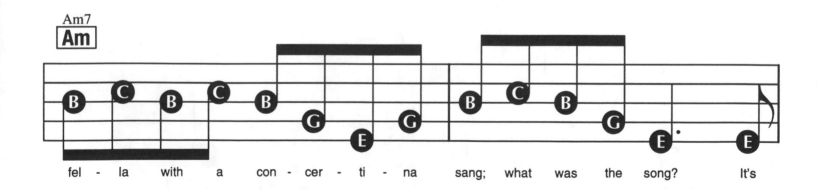

fel-la with a con-cer-ti-na sang; what was the song? It's

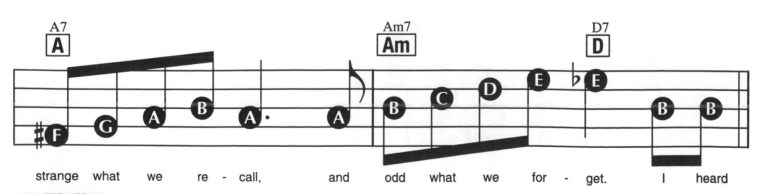

strange what we re-call, and odd what we for-get. I heard

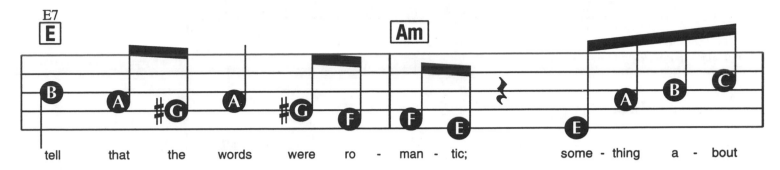

tell that the words were ro - man - tic; some - thing a - bout

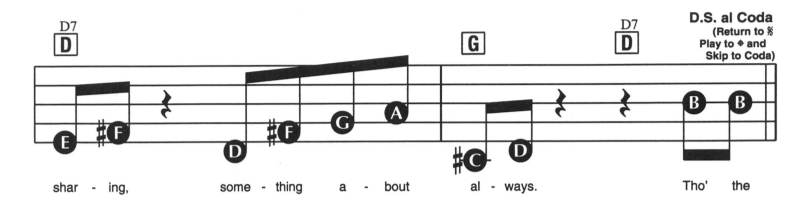

shar - ing, some - thing a - bout al - ways. Tho' the

D.S. al Coda
(Return to %
Play to ⊕ and
Skip to Coda)

CODA

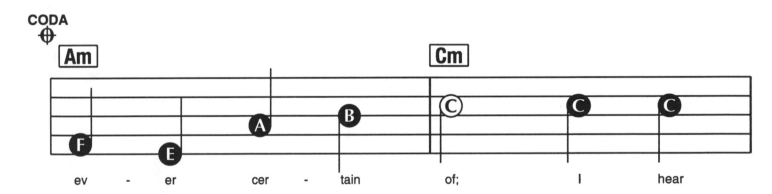

ev - er cer - tain of; I hear

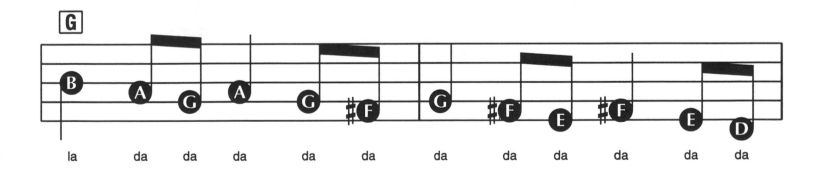

la da da da da da da da da da da da

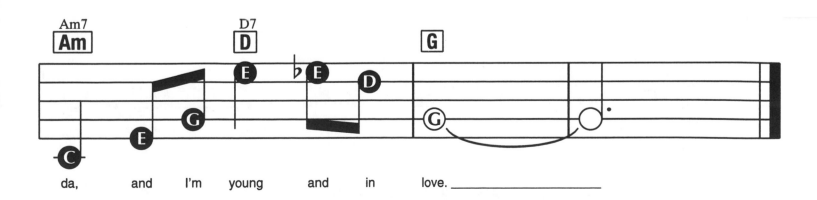

da, and I'm young and in love. _____

Sophisticated Lady

from SOPHISTICATED LADIES

Registration 7
Rhythm: Fox Trot or Swing

Words and Music by Duke Ellington,
Irving Mills and Mitchell Parish

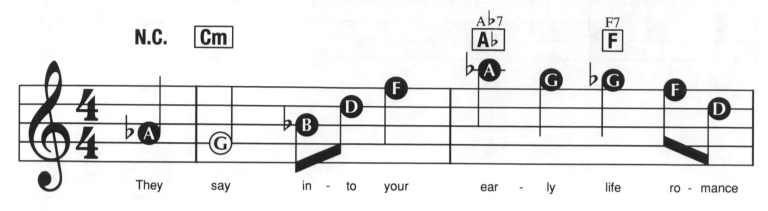

They say in - to your ear - ly life ro - mance

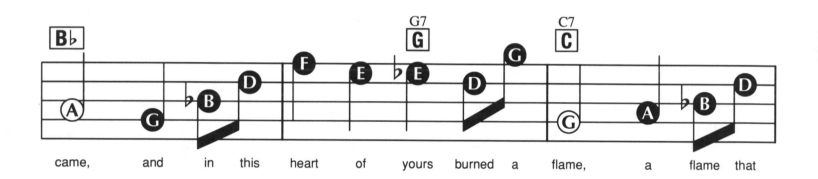

came, and in this heart of yours burned a flame, a flame that

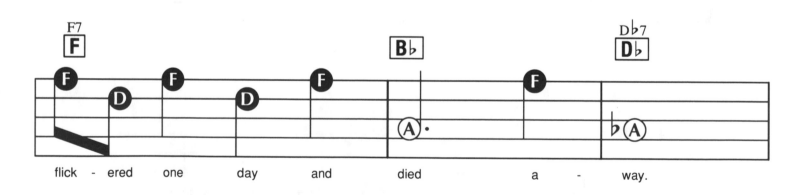

flick - ered one day and died a - way.

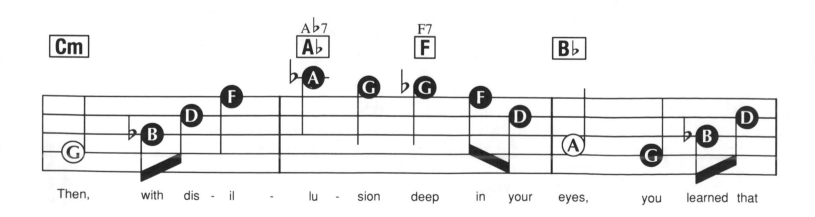

Then, with dis - il - lu - sion deep in your eyes, you learned that

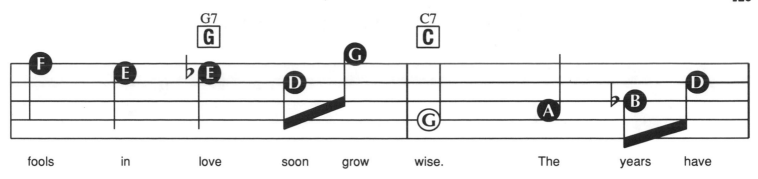

fools in love soon grow wise. The years have

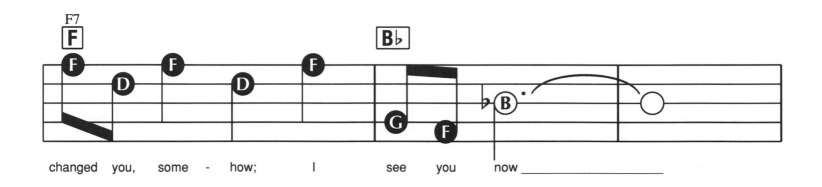

changed you, some - how; I see you now _____

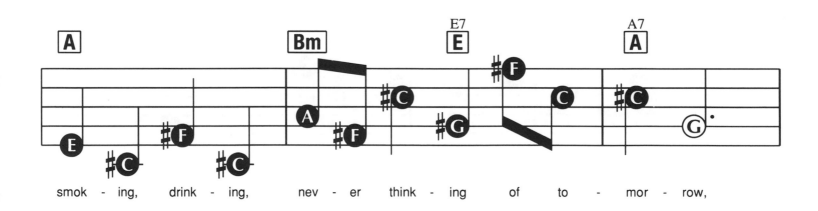

smok - ing, drink - ing, nev - er think - ing of to - mor - row,

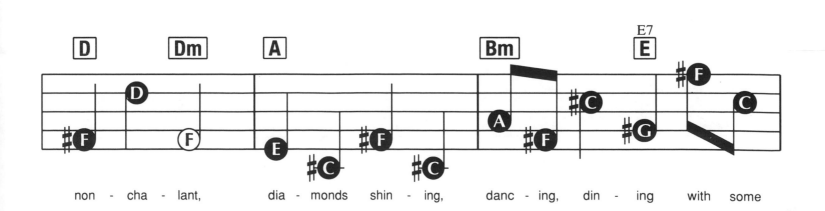

non - cha - lant, dia - monds shin - ing, danc - ing, din - ing with some

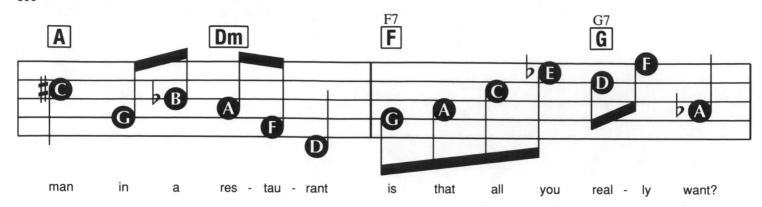

man in a res - tau - rant is that all you real - ly want?

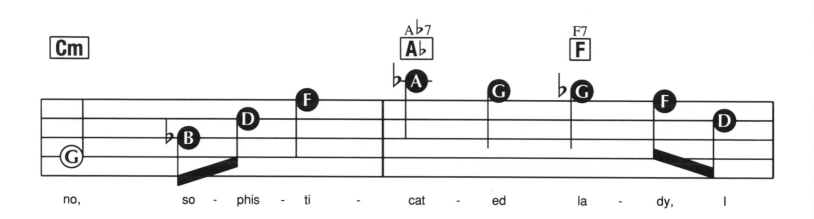

no, so - phis - ti - cat - ed la - dy, I

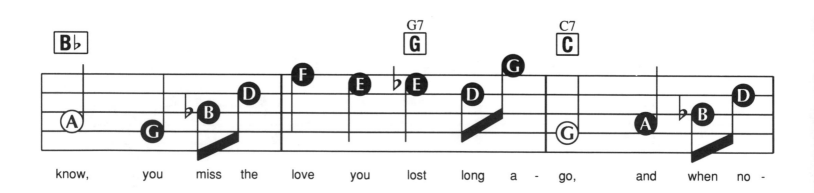

know, you miss the love you lost long a - go, and when no -

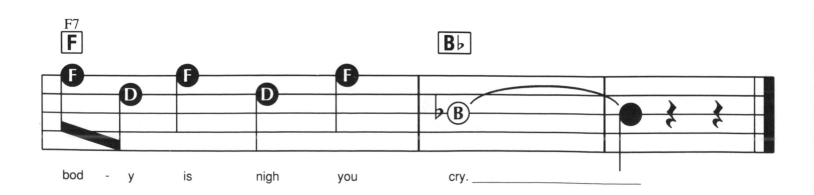

bod - y is nigh you cry. _____

Tell Me on a Sunday
from SONG AND DANCE

Registration 9
Rhythm: Pops or 8 Beat

Music by Andrew Lloyd Webber
Lyrics by Don Black

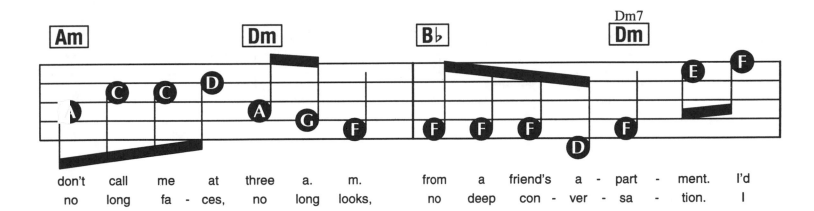

Don't write a let - ter when you want to leave,
Let me down ea - sy no big song and dance,

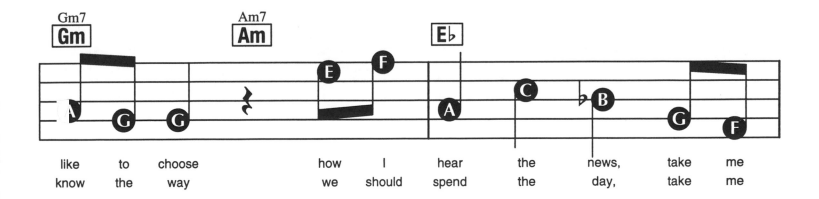

don't call me at three a. m. from a friend's a - part - ment. I'd
no long fa - ces, no long looks, no deep con - ver - sa - tion. I

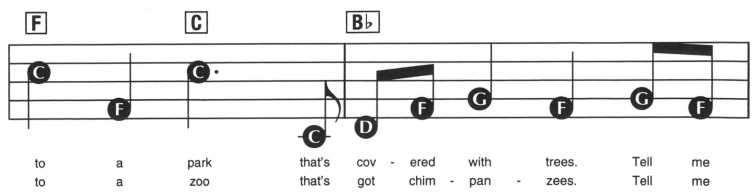

like to choose how I hear the news, take me
know the way we should spend the day, take me

to a park that's cov - ered with trees. Tell me
to a zoo that's got chim - pan - zees. Tell me

132

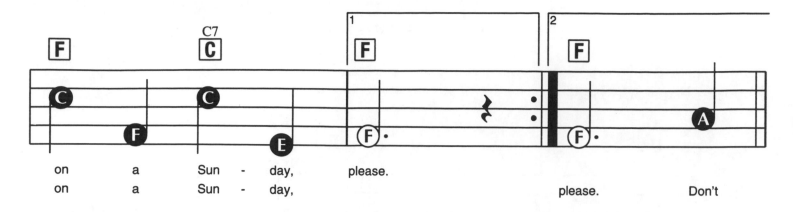

on a Sun - day, please.
on a Sun - day, please. Don't

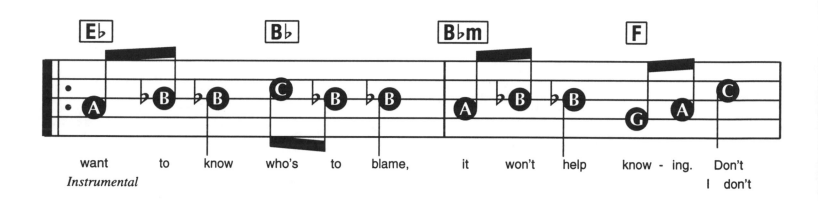

want to know who's to blame, it won't help know - ing. Don't
Instrumental
I don't

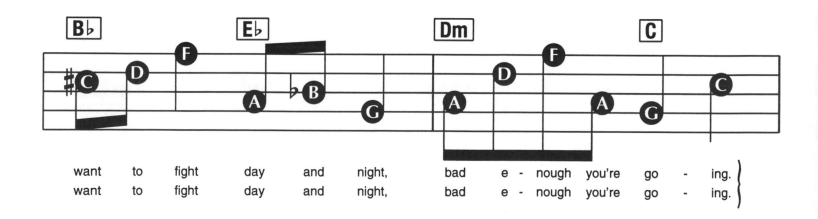

want to fight day and night, bad e - nough you're go - ing.
want to fight day and night, bad e - nough you're go - ing.

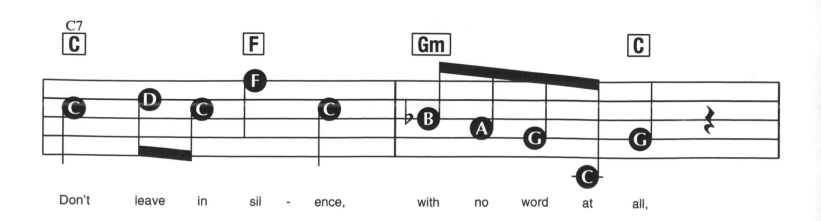

Don't leave in sil - ence, with no word at all,

don't get drunk and slam the door, that's no way to end this. I

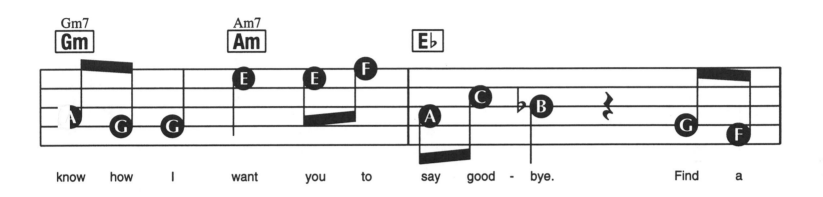

know how I want you to say good - bye. Find a

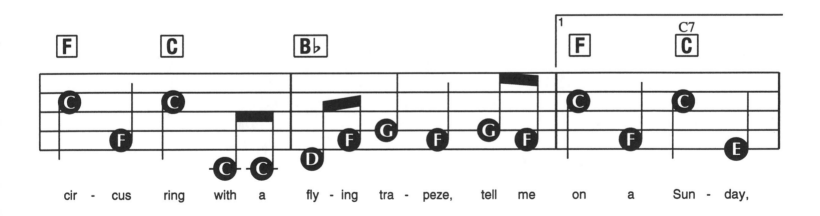

cir - cus ring with a fly - ing tra - peze, tell me on a Sun - day,

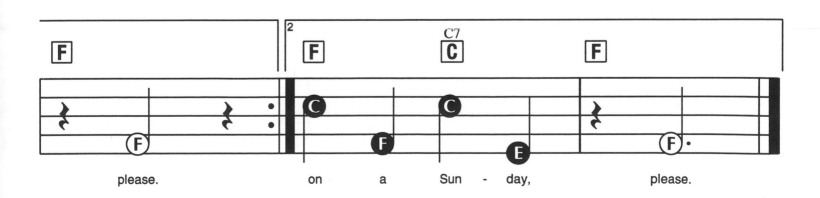

please. on a Sun - day, please.

The Surrey with the Fringe on Top
from OKLAHOMA!

Registration 7
Rhythm: Fox Trot or Ballad

Lyrics by Oscar Hammerstein II
Music by Richard Rodgers

Chicks and ducks and geese bet - ter scur - ry
Watch that fringe and see how it flut - ters

out in the sur - rey,
high step - pin' strut - ters.

When I take you
Nos - ey pokes - 'll

out in the sur - rey with the
peek in thru' their shut - ters and their

1. fringe on top!
2. eyes will pop! The

wheels are yel - ler, the up - hol - ster - y's brown, The dash - board's gen - u - ine

leath - er, with is - in - glass cur - tains y' can roll right down, in

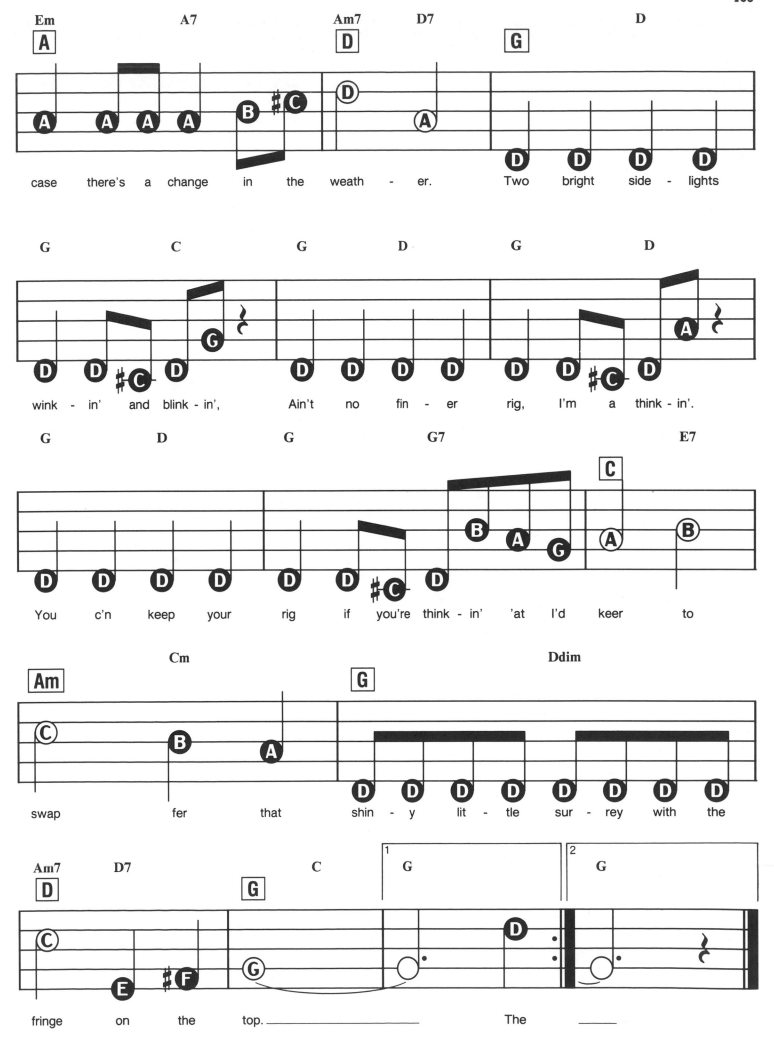

There's No Business Like Show Business

from the Stage Production ANNIE GET YOUR GUN

Registration 2
Rhythm: Fox Trot

Words and Music by
Irving Berlin

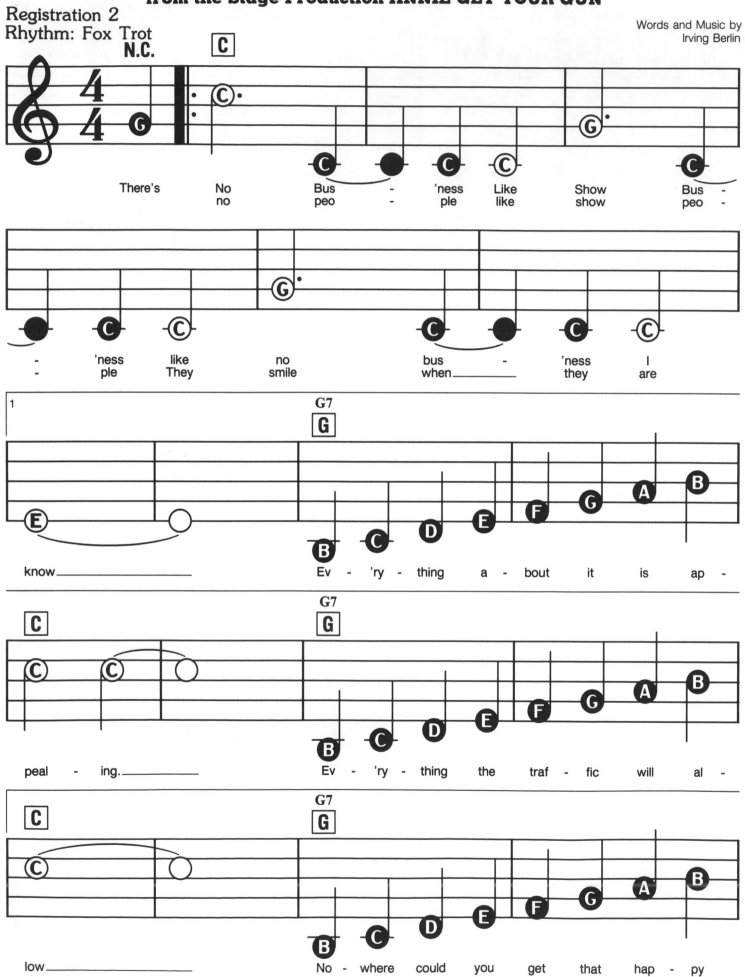

137

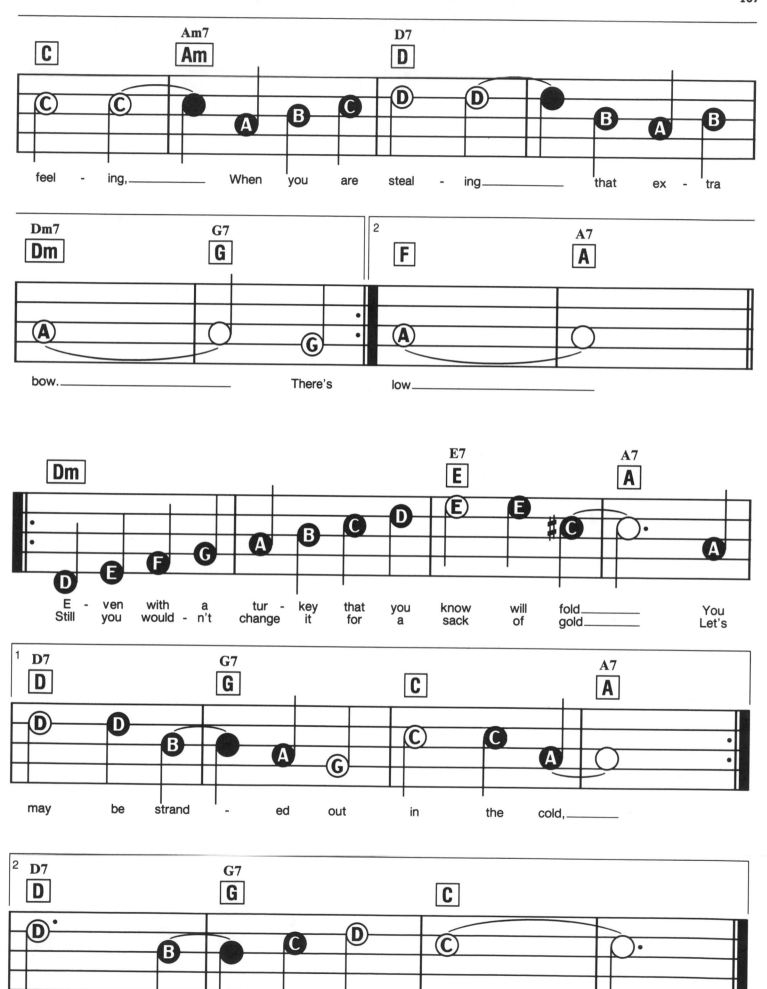

Turn Back, O Man
from the Musical GODSPELL

Registration 8
Rhythm: Swing or Shuffle

Words and Music by
Stephen Schwartz

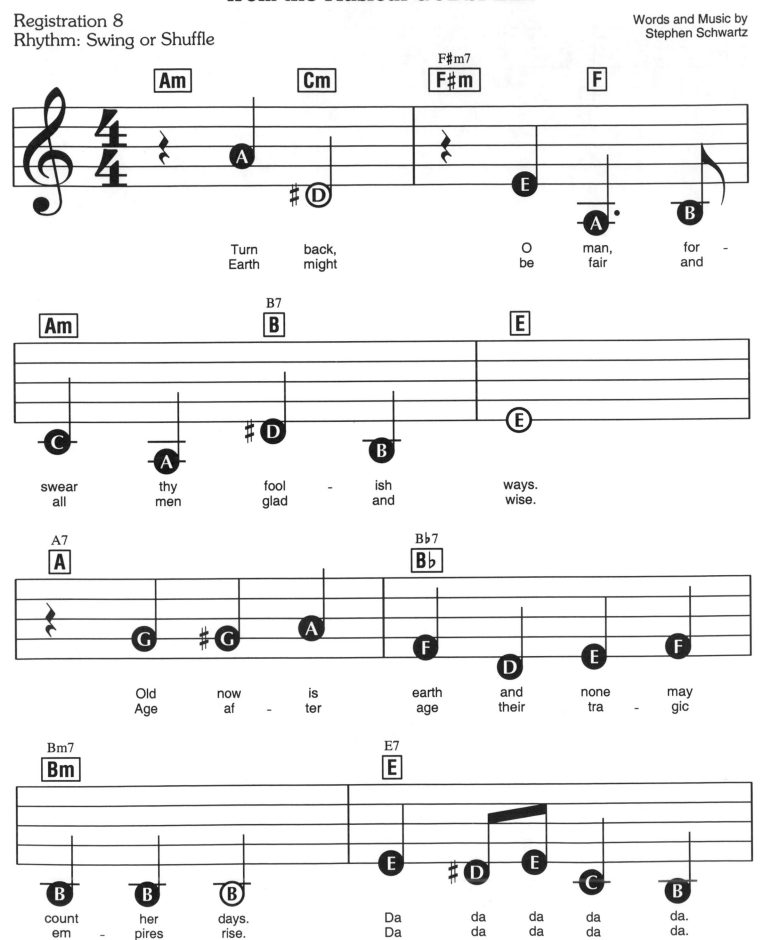

139

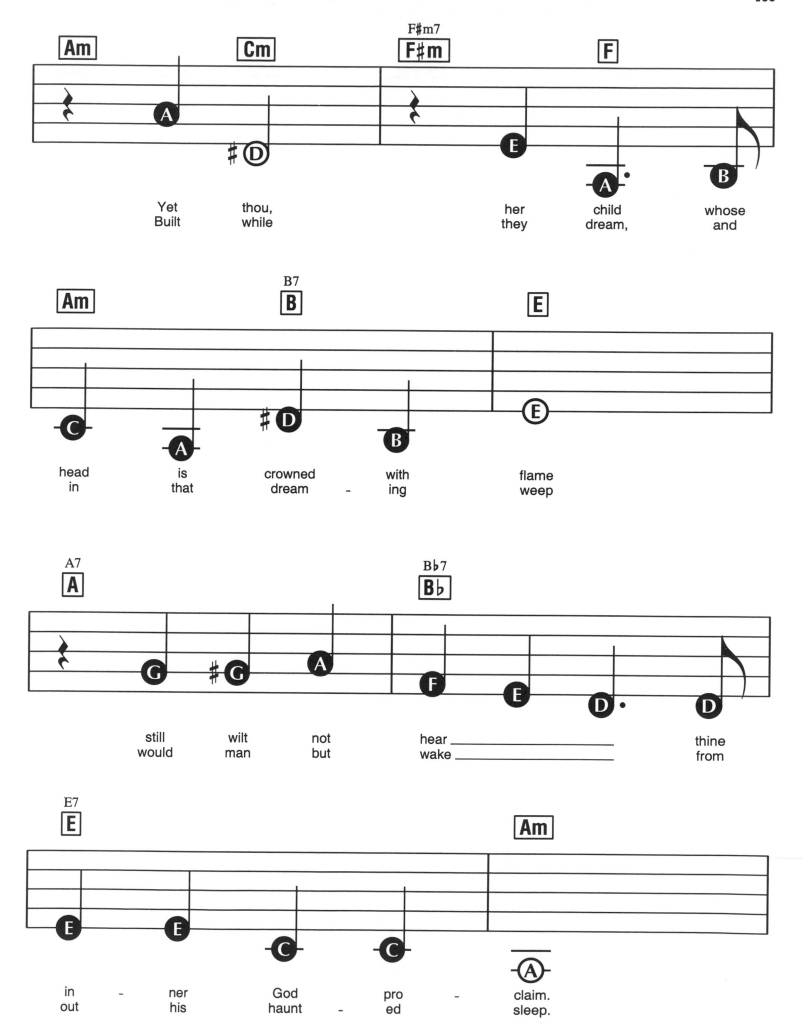

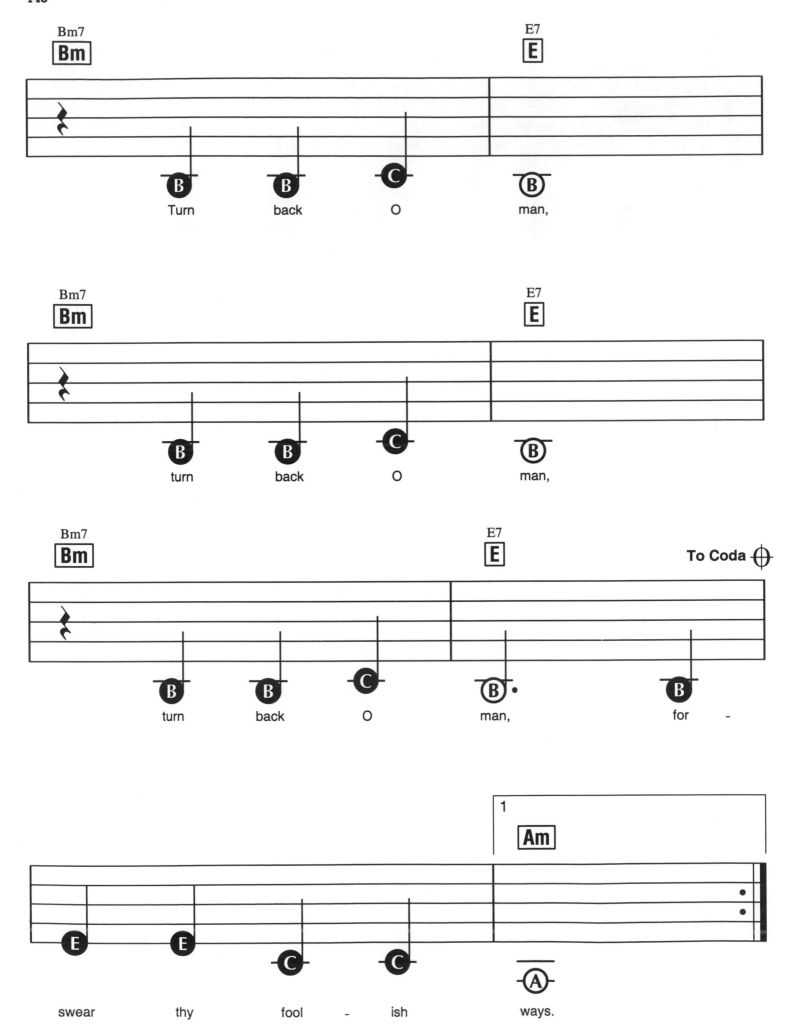

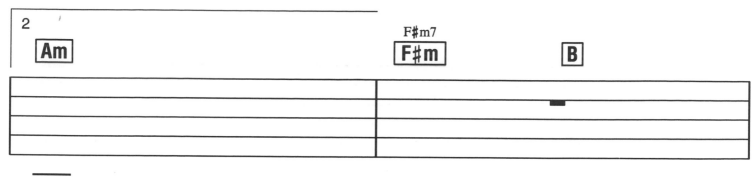

ways.

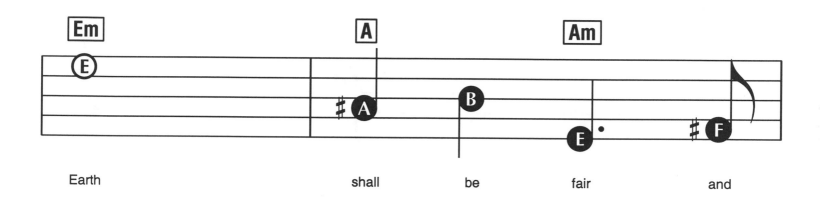

Earth   shall   be   fair   and

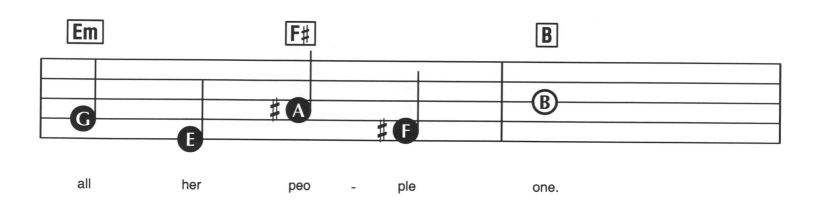

all   her   peo - ple   one.

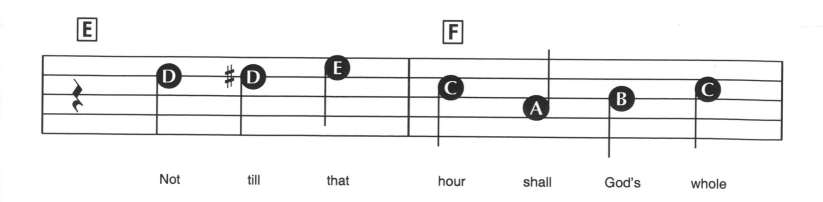

Not   till   that   hour   shall   God's   whole

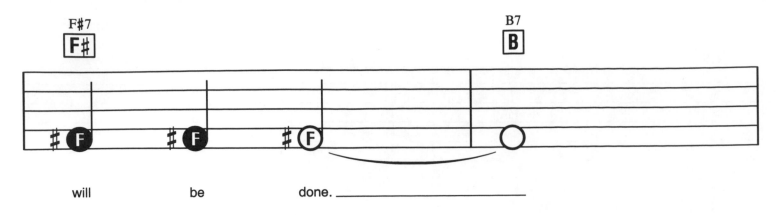

will   be   done. _____

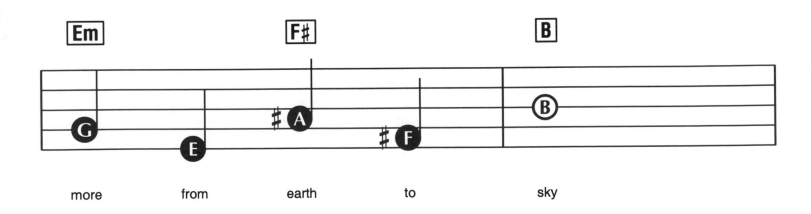

Now,   e - ven   now,   once

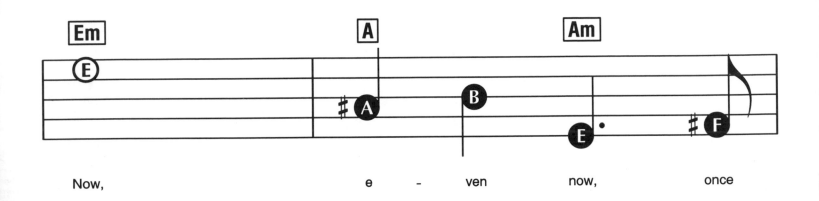

more   from   earth   to   sky

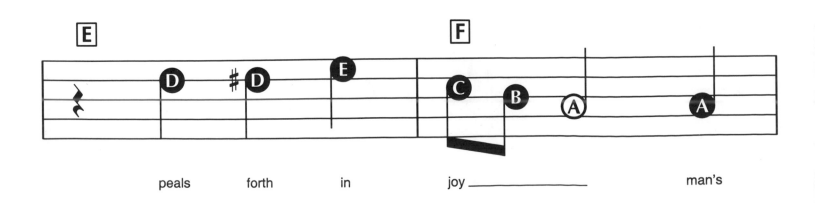

peals   forth   in   joy _____ man's

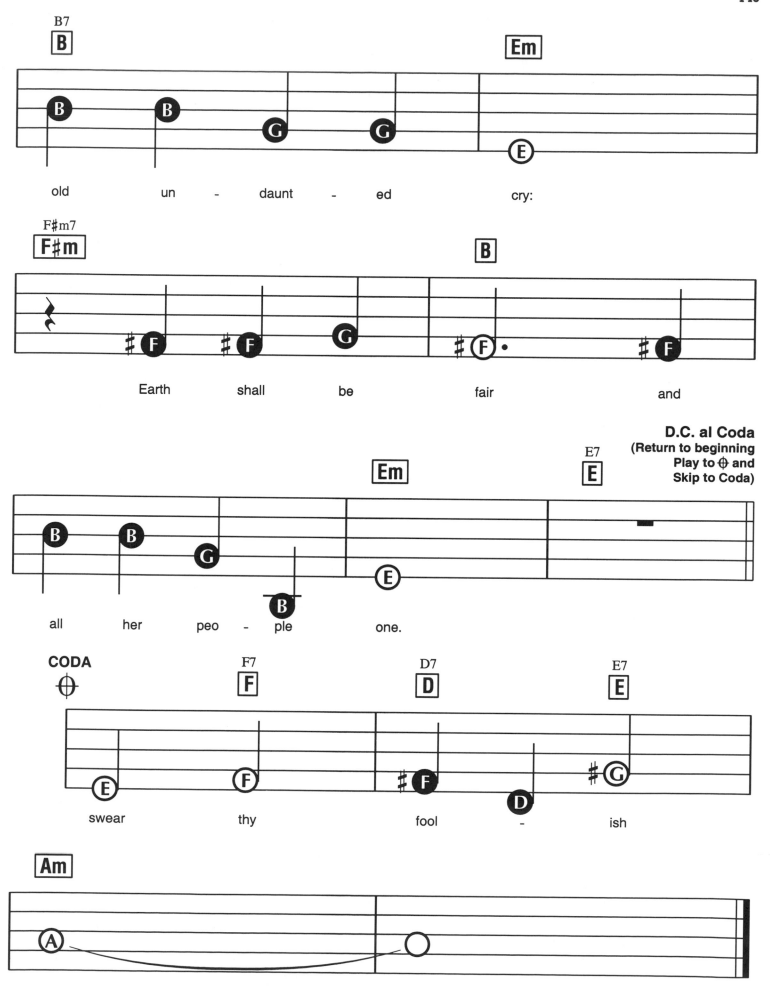

They Call the Wind Maria

from PAINT YOUR WAGON

Registration 1
Rhythm: Country

Words by Alan Jay Lerner
Music by Frederick Loewe

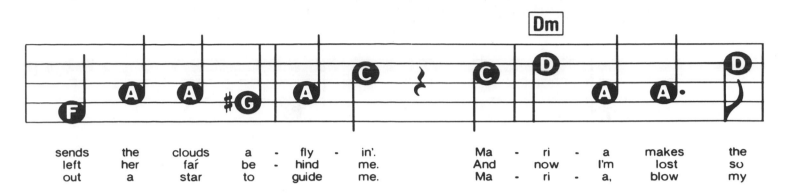

sends the clouds a - fly - in'.
left her far be - hind me.
out a star to guide me.

Ma - ri - a makes the
And now I'm lost so
Ma - ri - a, blow my

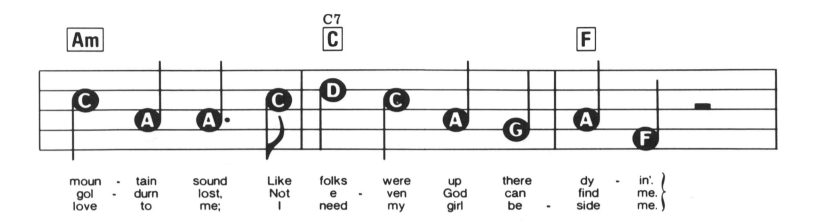

moun - tain sound; Like folks were up there dy - in'.
gol - durn lost, Not e - ven God can find me.
love to me; I need my girl be - side me.

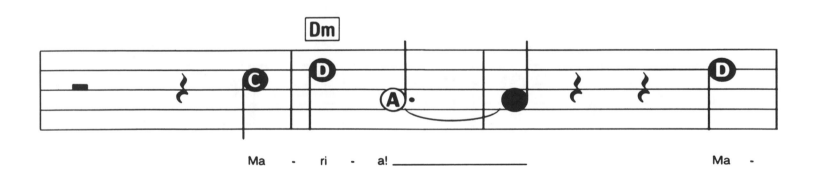

Ma - ri - a! _____ Ma -

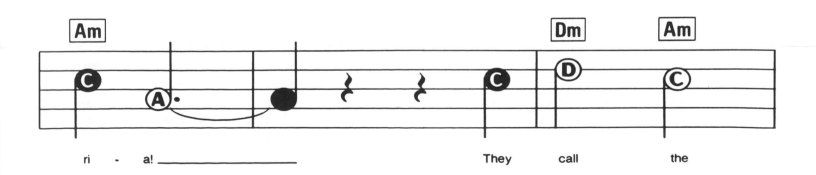

ri - a! _____ They call the

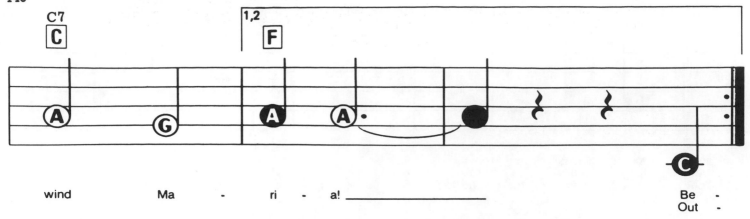

wind   Ma - ri - a! _____   Be -
                                                                                Out -

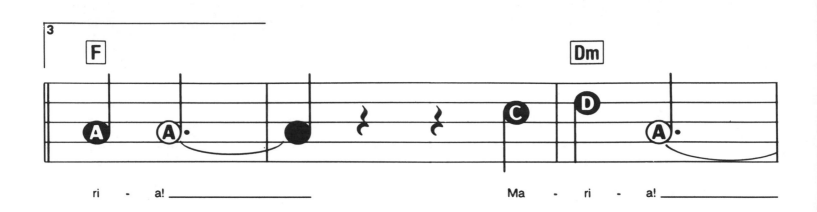

ri - a! _____   Ma - ri - a! _____

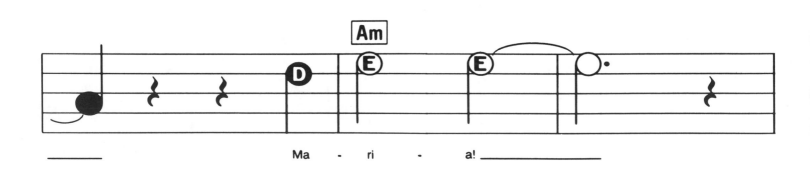

_____   Ma - ri - a! _____

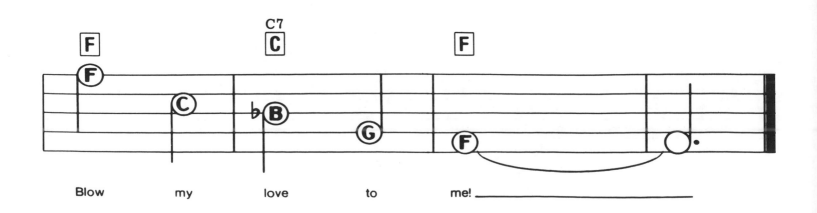

Blow   my   love   to   me! _____

Together Wherever We Go

from GYPSY

Registration 5
Rhythm: Fox Trot or Pops

Words by Stephen Sondheim
Music by Jule Styne

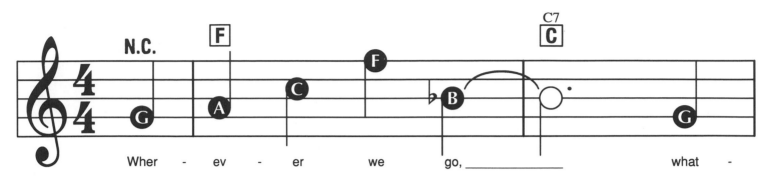

Wher - ev - er we go, _____ what -

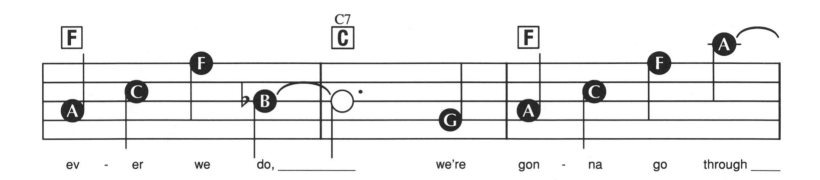

ev - er we do, _____ we're gon - na go through _____

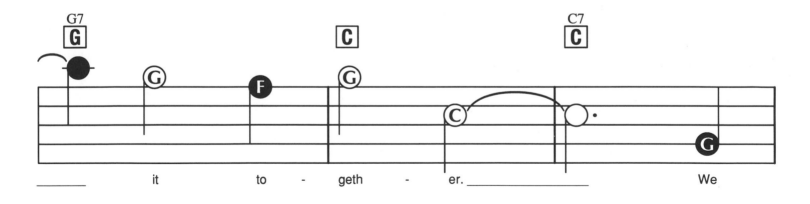

_____ it to - geth - er. _____ We

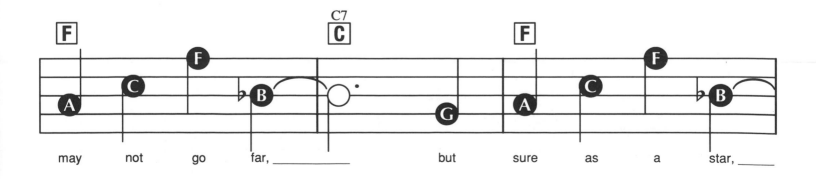

may not go far, _____ but sure as a star, _____

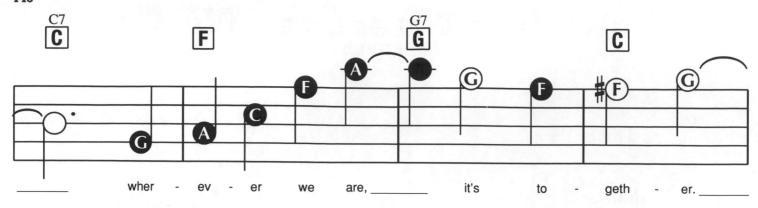

wher - ev - er we are, _____ it's to - geth - er. _____

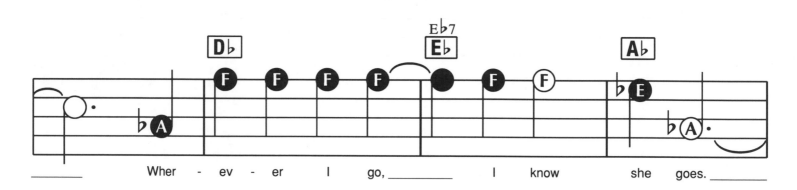

Wher - ev - er I go, _____ I know he goes. _____

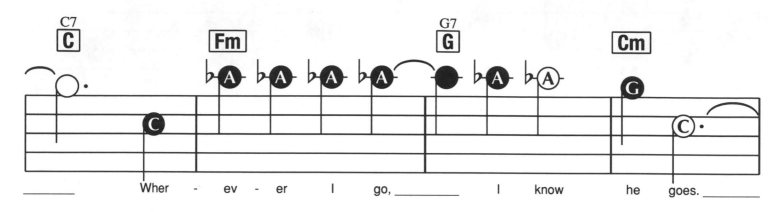

Wher - ev - er I go, _____ I know she goes. _____

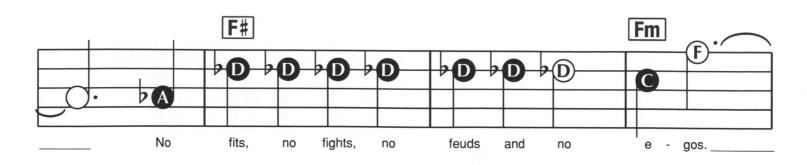

No fits, no fights, no feuds and no e - gos. _____

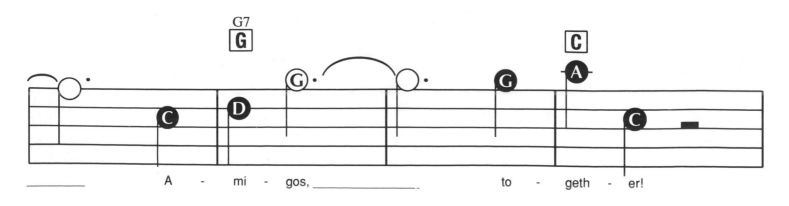

A - mi - gos, _____ to - geth - er!

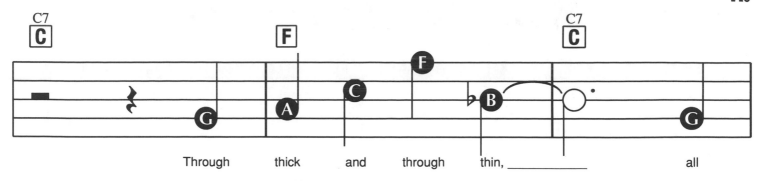

Through thick and through thin, _____ all

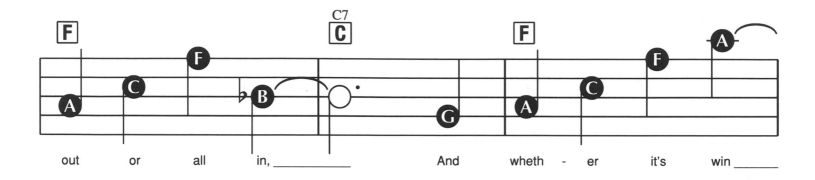

out or all in, _____ And wheth - er it's win _____

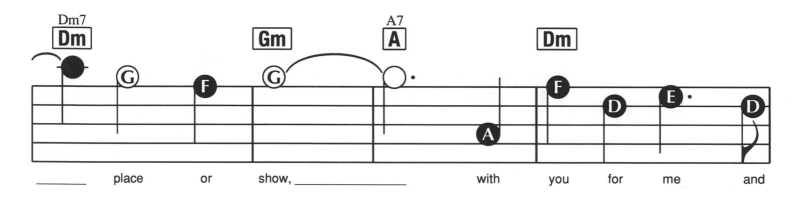

_____ place or show, _____ with you for me and

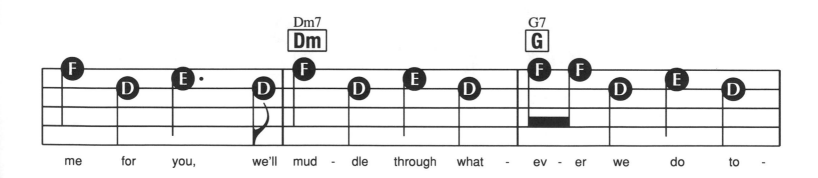

me for you, we'll mud - dle through what - ev - er we do to -

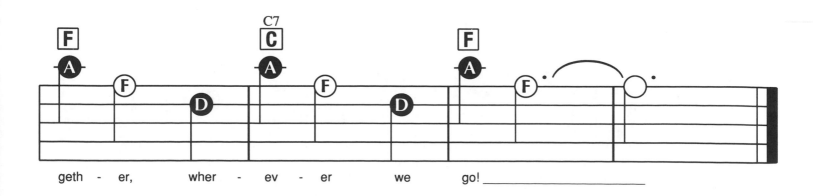

geth - er, wher - ev - er we go! _____

Who Can I Turn To
(When Nobody Needs Me)
from THE ROAR OF THE GREASEPAINT – THE SMELL OF THE CROWD

Registration 10
Rhythm: Ballad or Fox Trot

Words and Music by Leslie Bricusse
and Anthony Newley

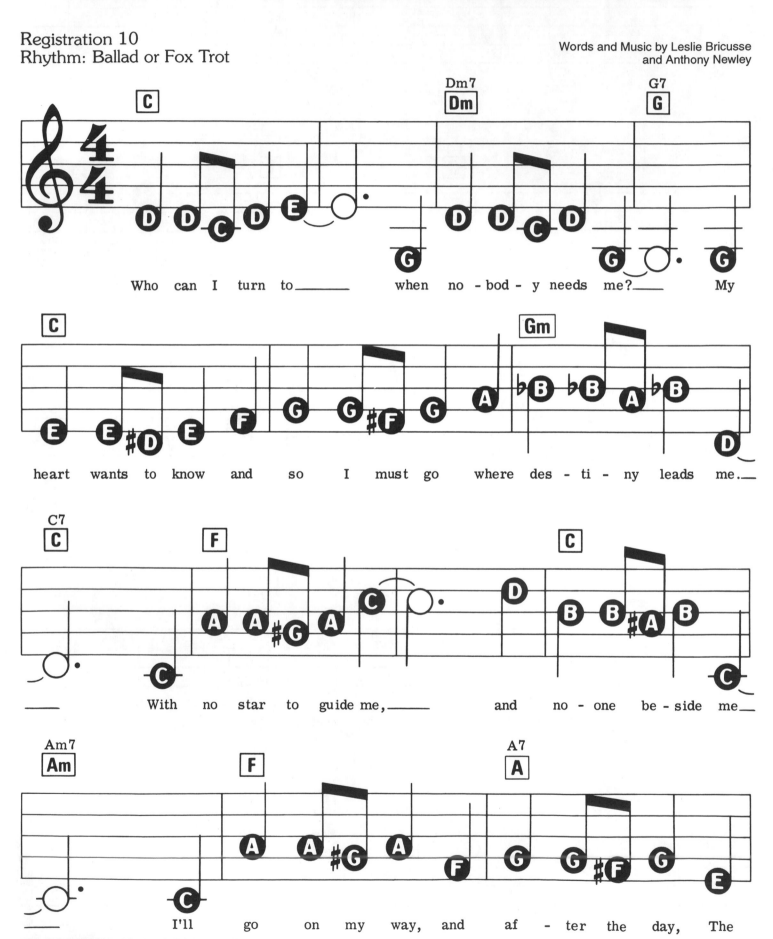

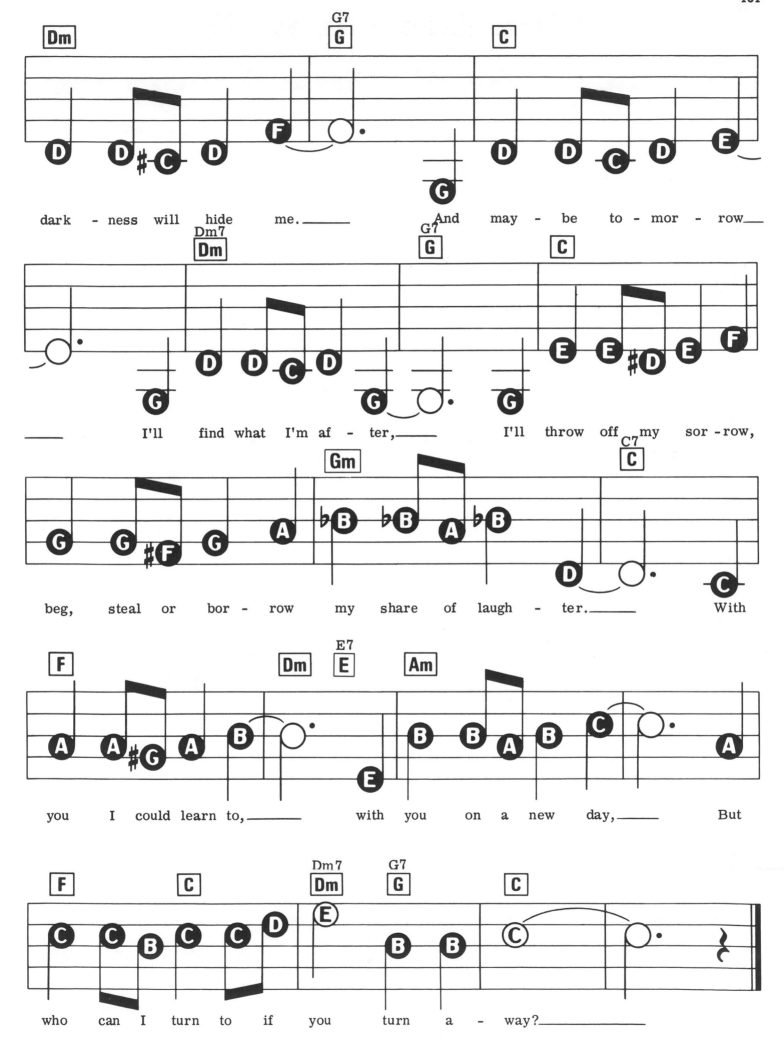

Willkommen
from the Musical CABARET

Registration 7
Rhythm: Swing or Jazz

Words by Fred Ebb
Music by John Kander

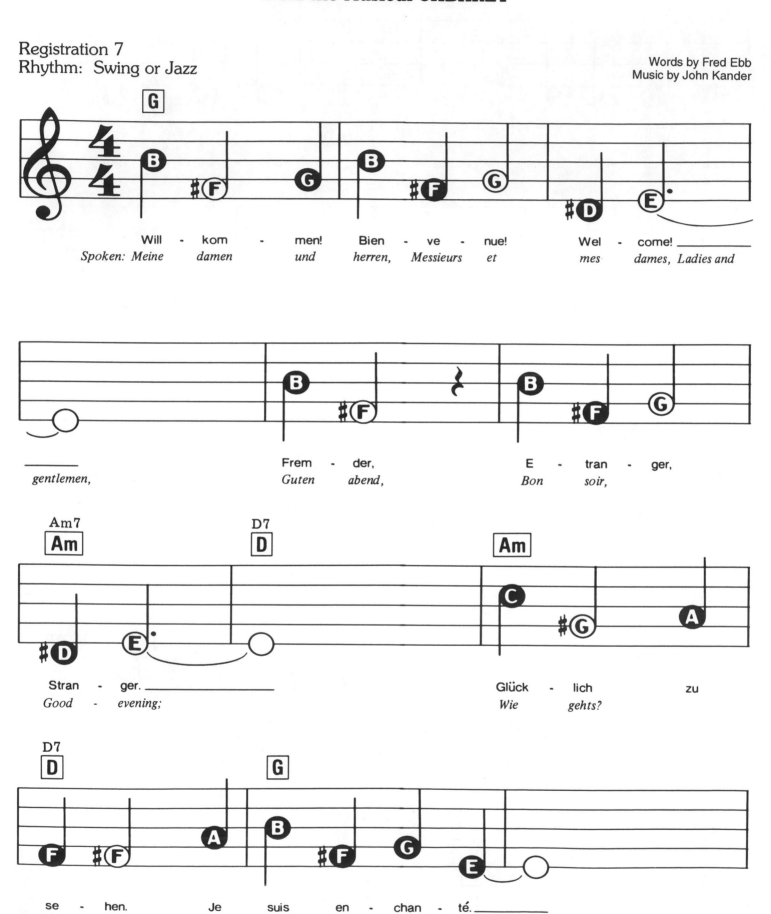

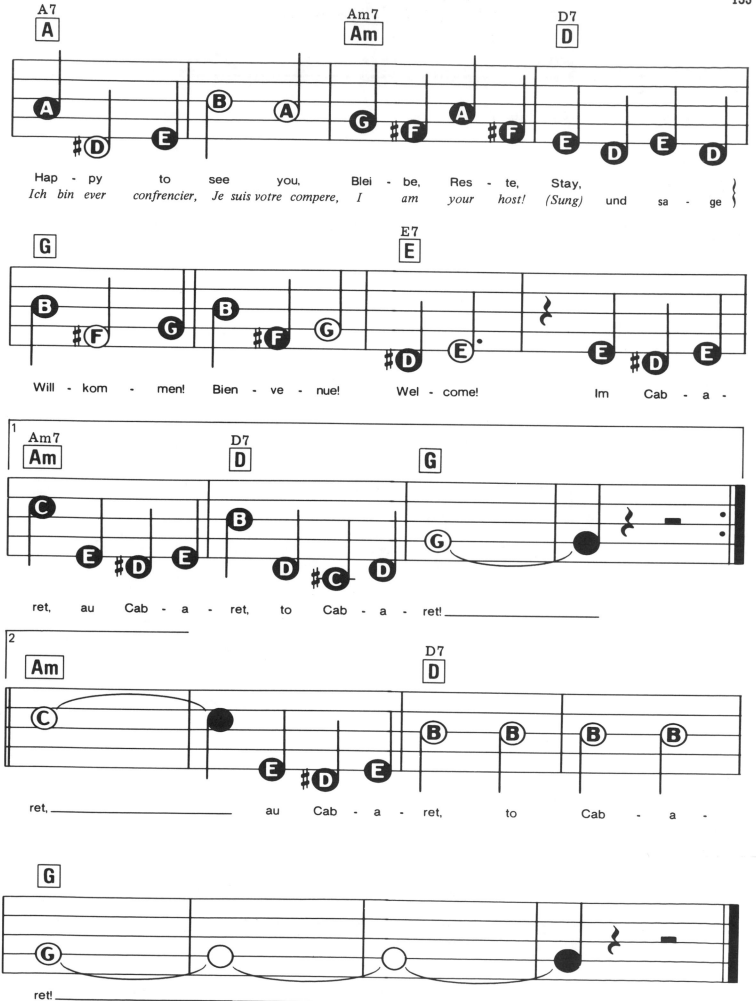

Wishing You Were Somehow Here Again

from THE PHANTOM OF THE OPERA

Music by Andrew Lloyd Webber
Lyrics by Charles Hart
Additional Lyrics by Richard Stilgoe

Registration 3
Rhythm: 8 Beat or Rock Ballad

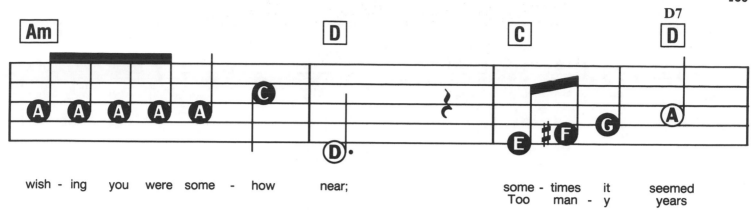

wish - ing you were some - how near;
some - times it seemed
Too man - y years

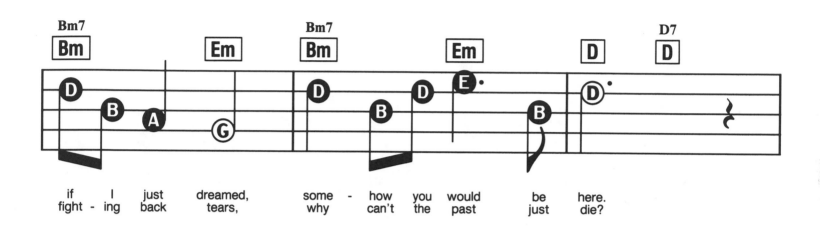

if I just dreamed,
fight - ing back tears,
some - how you would be here.
why can't the past just die?

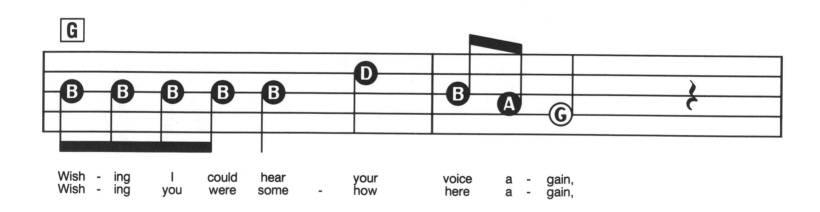

Wish - ing I could hear your voice a - gain,
Wish - ing you were some - how here a - gain,

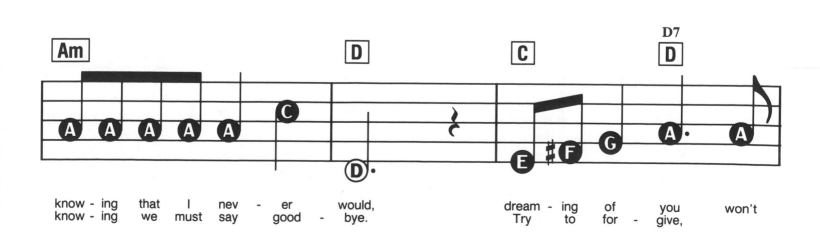

know - ing that I nev - er would,
know - ing we must say good - bye.
dream - ing of you won't
Try to for - give,

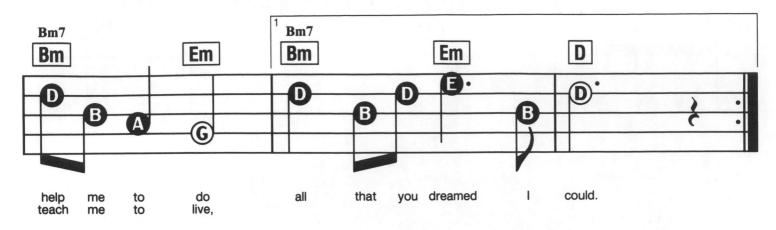

help me to do all that you dreamed I could.
teach me to live,

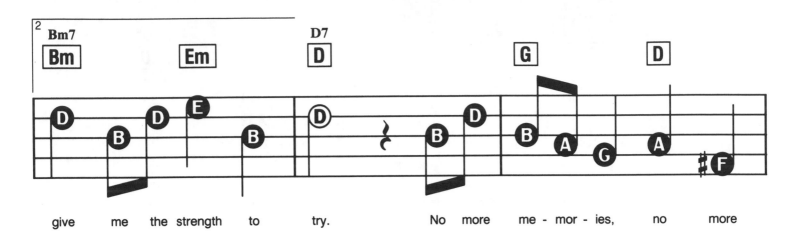

give me the strength to try. No more me - mor - ies, no more

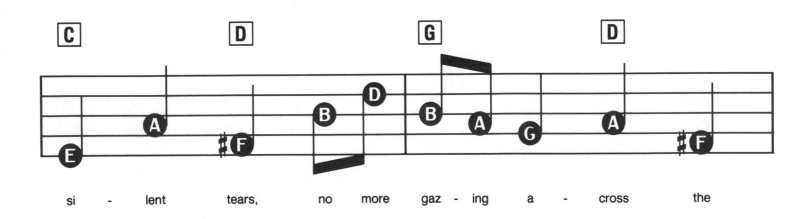

si - lent tears, no more gaz - ing a - cross the

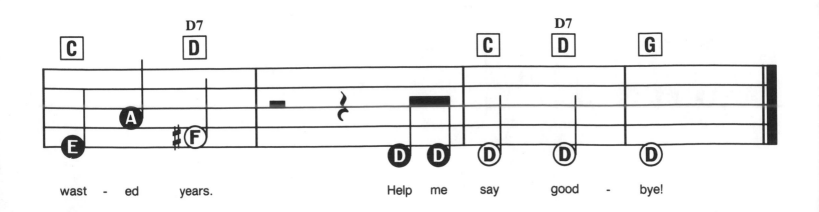

wast - ed years. Help me say good - bye!

A Wonderful Guy
from SOUTH PACIFIC

Registration 4
Rhythm: Waltz

Lyrics by Oscar Hammerstein II
Music by Richard Rodgers

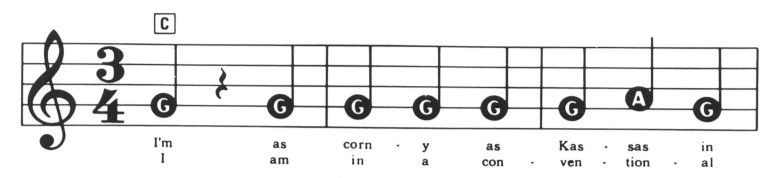

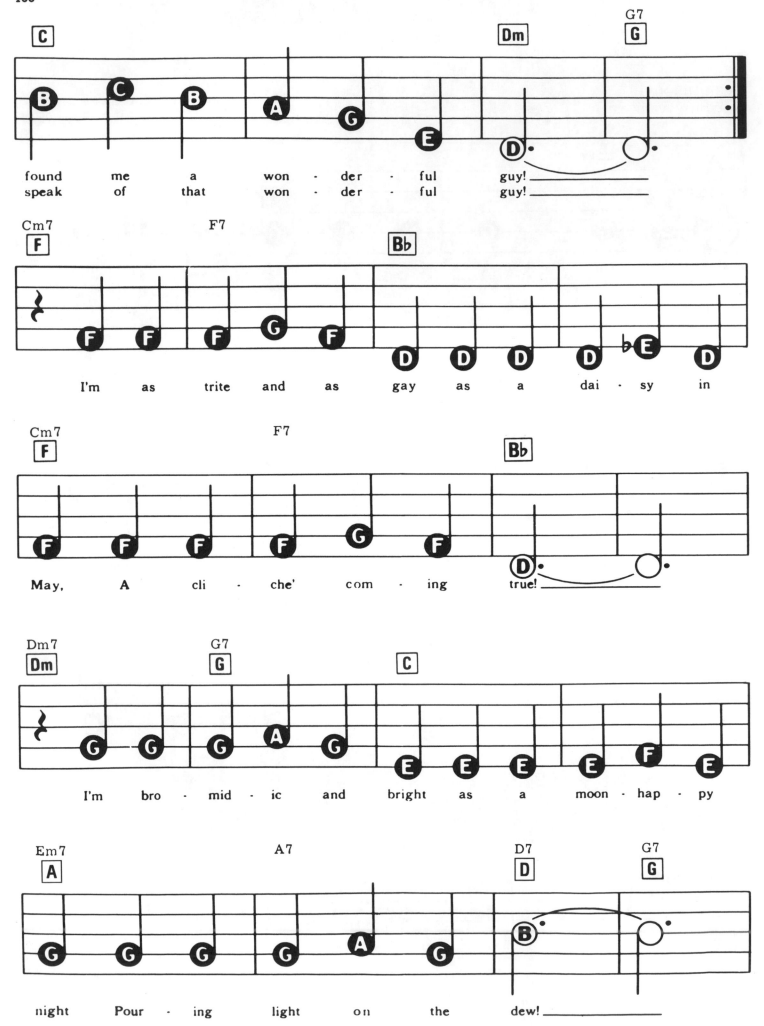

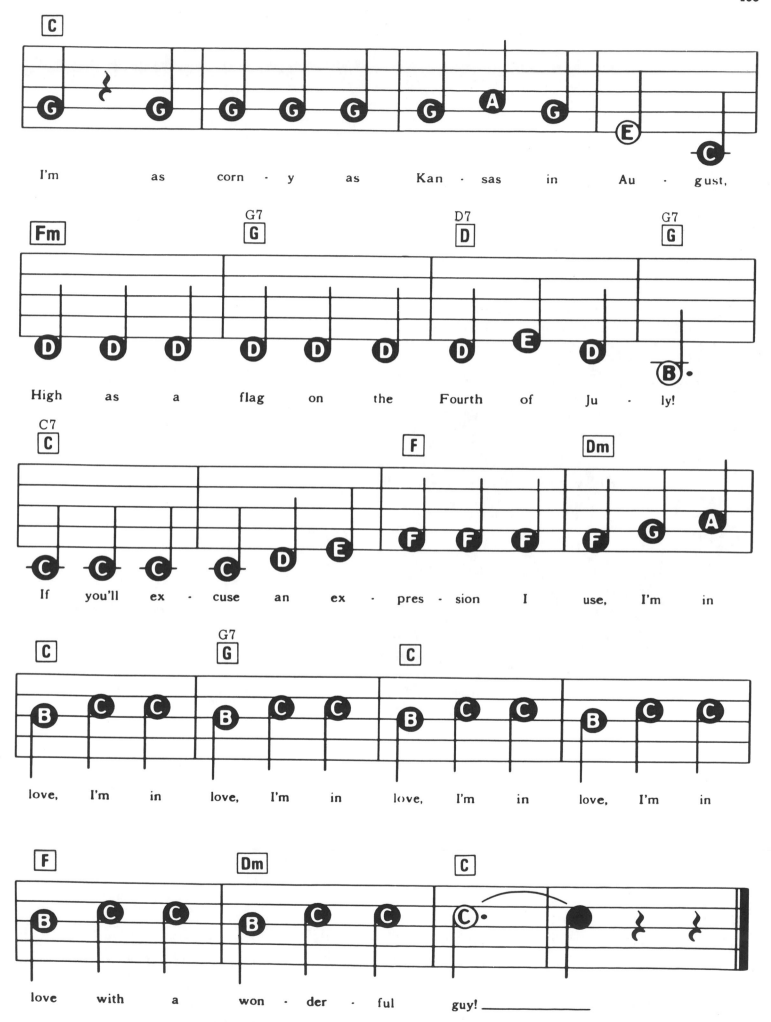

THE TWENTIETH CENTURY SERIES
the 20th Century

This beautiful series of songbooks celebrates the first century of recorded music and the many genres of music that evolved over 100 years. Each book is arranged in Hal Leonard's patented E-Z Play® Today notation.

THE 20TH CENTURY: BROADWAY

A comprehensive overview of 100 years of Broadway musicals with over 50 songs, including: As If We Never Said Goodbye • Beauty and the Beast • Brotherhood of Man • Cabaret • Close Every Door • Hello, Dolly! • The Impossible Dream (The Quest) • On My Own • One • Seasons of Love • Some Enchanted Evening • Song on the Sand (La Da Da Da) • The Surrey with the Fringe on Top • and more!

_____00100128 E-Z Play Today #402 ....$12.95

THE 20TH CENTURY: COUNTRY MUSIC

Over 50 country classics representative of a century's worth of music, including: Always on My Mind • Amazed • Blue Eyes Crying in the Rain • Blue Moon of Kentucky • Boot Scootin' Boogie • Breathe • Crazy • Folsom Prison Blues • Friends in Low Places • Hey, Good Lookin' • Jambalaya (On the Bayou) • King of the Road • Lucille • Ring of Fire • Your Cheatin' Heart • and more.

_____00100129 E-Z Play Today #403 ....$12.95

THE 20TH CENTURY: JAZZ STANDARDS

Over 50 jazz standards that set the tone for the 20th century, including: All or Nothing at All • Autumn in New York • Body and Soul • Brazil • Caravan • Don't Get Around Much Anymore • Harlem Nocturne • How Deep Is the Ocean (How High Is the Sky) • In the Mood • Manhattan • Misty • Route 66 • Satin Doll • Skylark • Star Dust • Stella by Starlight • Take the "A" Train • and more!

_____00100132 E-Z Play Today #404 ....$12.95

THE 20TH CENTURY: LOVE SONGS

Over 50 of the century's favorite love songs, including: Always in My Heart (Siempre en mi corazón) • And I Love Her • Cherish • (They Long to Be) Close to You • Just the Way You Are • Make It with You • (You Make Me Feel Like) A Natural Woman • Star Dust • Unexpected Song • The Very Thought of You • When I Fall in Love • Wonderful Tonight • You Are the Sunshine of My Life • You've Got a Friend • more.

_____00100133 E-Z Play Today #405 ....$12.95

THE 20TH CENTURY: MOVIE MUSIC

Over 50 of the century's best songs from the cinema, including: Change the World • Chariots of Fire • Do You Know Where You're Going To? • Endless Love • I Will Remember You • Moon River • My Heart Will Go On (Love Theme from 'Titanic') • Supercalifragilisticexpialidocious • Tears in Heaven • Unchained Melody • The Way We Were • more.

_____00100130 E-Z Play Today #406 ....$12.95

THE 20TH CENTURY: THE ROCK ERA

Over 50 songs that defined the rock era, including: Baby Love • Dust in the Wind • Eleanor Rigby • Fire and Rain • Heartbreak Hotel • Imagine • Oh, Pretty Woman • Piano Man • Time After Time • Twist and Shout • Wild Thing • more.

_____00100131 E-Z Play Today #407 ....$12.95

FOR MORE INFORMATION, SEE YOUR LOCAL MUSIC DEALER, OR WRITE TO:

HAL•LEONARD® CORPORATION
7777 W. BLUEMOUND RD. P.O. BOX 13819 MILWAUKEE, WI 53213

Visit Hal Leonard Online at
www.halleonard.com

Prices, contents, and availability subject to change without notice.